SPECTRUM
Writing

Grade 6

Published by Spectrum
an imprint of Carson-Dellosa Publishing LLC
Greensboro, NC

Spectrum
An imprint of Carson-Dellosa Publishing LLC
P.O. Box 35665
Greensboro, NC 27425 USA

ISBN 0-7696-5286-7

2 3 4 5 6 7 8 9 10 QDB 16 15 14 13 12 11 10   335107811

Table of Contents Grade 6

Table of Contents, continued

Chapter 1
Lesson 1 Main Ideas and Details

A paragraph has a main idea. The main idea is what the paragraph is all about. In most paragraphs, the main idea is actually stated in the paragraph. That statement is called the topic sentence. A topic sentence may be anywhere in a paragraph, but most often it is either the first sentence or the last.

In the paragraph below, the topic sentence is the first sentence. Write it below.

My grandmother is one of those people who has her holiday shopping done by September. She picks out gifts when she and Grandpa travel. She also goes to local stores when they have sales during the summer. In December, when we're all feeling too busy, Grandma is at home baking cookies.

My grandmother is one of those people who has her holiday shopping done by September.

The other sentences include details that support, or tell about, the main idea. Write two details from the paragraph.

She picks out gifts when she and grandpa travel.
She also goes to local stores when they have sales during the summer.

Lesson 1 Main Ideas and Details

Not all paragraphs have a topic sentence. Sometimes, writers leave it out. The paragraph still has a main idea, but the writer chooses not to state the main idea in the paragraph. That means the main idea is implied. Here is an example.

All of the stores were crowded yesterday. They weren't necessarily full of people, though. Everywhere I went, there were special displays. I guess they figure that if you trip over the display, you're more likely to buy something. That's not how it worked for me. I was so annoyed that I cut my shopping trip short and went for a walk in the park.

What is the main idea of the paragraph above?

The stores were crowded yesterday.

How do you feel about shopping? Choose one of these sentences as a topic sentence for a paragraph:

I hate shopping.

(I like shopping, but only for myself.)

I would like to be a professional shopper.

Now, write a paragraph in which you support your main idea with details. Remember to choose just one topic sentence. Decide whether you will put it at the beginning, in the middle, or at the end of the paragraph.

I like shopping, but only for myself.
When I am getting dragged along for
someone else's shopping I get really bored.
As for shopping for me it is pretty easy
and I never have nothing to do. Whether
it's from clothes to accessories shopping for
myself is what I like to do the most.

NAME _Samiksha Kale_

Lesson 2 Staying on Topic

Most of the details in this picture fit the main idea, but one does not. What is it? Describe the detail that does not fit.

The movie stand does not fit, in the forest scene.

Now, write a sentence that states the main idea of the picture. (Remember to ignore that detail that doesn't fit.)

A hiker is hiking in a forest.

Normally, all of the details in a picture fit the main idea. The same should be true of a paragraph: all of the details should fit the main idea. In other words, each sentence must stay on topic.

Here is a good paragraph. It starts out with a topic sentence. Then, each sentence gives details about, or supports, the topic sentence.

Many people say they would rather not live in a city, but few people actually make the move to the country. In a recent survey, 66% of the adults polled said they longed for a rural lifestyle. However, only about 2% of those people said they had actually taken steps toward such a move. Steps they had taken included searching for real estate and inquiring about job opportunities in rural communities.

NAME Samiksha Kole

Lesson 2 Staying on Topic

The following paragraph contains a sentence that is not on topic. Read the paragraph and underline the topic sentence. Draw a line through the sentence that does not support the topic sentence. Then, list two details that do support the topic sentence.

For a city kid, country life can be a little alarming. I learned that on a recent visit to see my aunt and uncle. As we pulled up in front of their house, a possum crossed the driveway. I let out a yell. I thought it was a huge rat! ~~Possums are not even in the same family as rats.~~ After we all settled down from that, my aunt's cat deposited a dead mouse on the doorstep. Aunt Terry calmly picked it up by the tail and tossed it into the bushes.

Detail: I thought is was a huge rat

Detail: Aunt Terry calmly picked it up by the tail and tossed it into the bushes

Now, write your own paragraph about an experience you have had in the country or outdoors. Remember to stay on topic. Stick to one main idea and make sure that all of your detail sentences support that main idea. When you are finished, underline your topic sentence.

Since I am mostly an indoors kid, going outdoors can be a little of a fright. Once when I was outside I saw a lot of bees coming and going. I was terrified and tried to hide in the top of the playset that we had in our yard. One of the bees came under the playset and started making humming "Buzz" noises, I prayed to god to not let the bee come up to where I was hiding. Unfortunately, the bee came up, and even though it wasn't going to sting me I still ran into my house screaming.

Lesson 3 The Writing Process

Writers follow a plan when they write. They take certain steps, which make up the writing process. Following these five steps leads to better writing.

Step 1: Prewrite

This could also be called the "thinking and discovering" stage. Writers might choose a topic, or they might list everything they know about a topic already chosen. They might write down what they need to learn about a topic. Some also organize their ideas by making a chart or diagram.

Step 2: Draft

Writers put their ideas on paper. This first draft should contain sentences and paragraphs. Good writers follow their prewriting ideas while writing the draft. There might be spelling and grammar mistakes in this draft. There might even be mistakes in facts or ideas and how they are organized. That's okay; there are three more steps.

Step 3: Revise

Writers change or fix their first draft. They move ideas around, put them in a different order, or add new ones. They make sure they used clear words and the sentences flow smoothly together. This is also the time to take out ideas that are not on topic.

Step 4: Proofread

Writers usually write a neat, new copy. Then, they look again to make sure everything is correct. They look especially for capital letters, end marks, punctuation, and misspelled words.

Step 5: Publish

Finally, writers make a final copy that has no mistakes. They are now ready to share their writing. That might mean mailing a letter, turning in a report, or posting a story on a bulletin board.

Lesson 3 The Writing Process

What does the writing process look like? Chase used the writing process to write a paragraph about Sacagawea. His writing steps below are out of order. Label each step with a number and the name of the step.

Step _4_ : _Proofread_

Sacagawea was about 19 years old when she began traveling with Lewis and Clark on their great expeditoin. Her husband, a French fur trader named Charbonneau, had been hired as an interpreter. Though Sacagawea was "only a woman" and had a baby, she went along. Historians agree that Sacagawea's role in negotiating with her own Shoshone people aided the expedition a great deal so, it is Sacagawea, not her husband, who becomes a hero.

Step _5_ : _Publish_

Sacagawea was about 19 years old when she began traveling with Lewis and Clark on their great expedition. Her husband, a French fur trader named Charbonneau, had been hired as an interpreter. Though Sacagawea was "only a woman" and had a baby, she went along. Historians agree that Sacagawea's role in negotiating with her own Shoshone people helped ensure the success of the expedition. So, it is Sacagawea, not her husband, who becomes a hero.

Step _1_ : _Prewrite_

Shoshone
with Lewis and Clark, starting in 1805
carried her baby
husband, Charbonneau, interpreter
about 1786 to 1812

Step _3_ : _Revise_

Sacagawea was about 19 years old, when she went with Lewis and Clark on their great expeditoin. Her husband, named Charbonneau, had been hired as an interpreter. Though Sacagawea was "only a woman" and had a baby, she went along Historians agree that Sacagawea's role in talking to her own Shoshone people aided the expedition a great deal, so, it is Sacagawea, not her husband, who becomes a hero.

Step _2_ : _Draft_

Sacagawea was about 19 years old, when she went with Lewis and Clark on their great expeditoin. Her husband, named Charbonneau, had been hired as an interpreter. Though Sacagawea was "only a woman" and had a baby, she went along Historians agree that Sacagawea's role in talking to her own Shoshone people aided the expedition a great deal, so, it is Sacagawea, not her husband, who becomes a hero.

Lesson 4 Purposes for Writing

When you are in school, you write assignments for your teachers. Beyond completing a school assignment, though, there are several basic purposes, or reasons, for writing. In general, they are as follows:

- to entertain
- to persuade
- to explain
- to inform

Writers use many forms of writing, such as friendly letters, reports, news articles, book reviews, and poems. For one form of writing, there might be different purposes. Here are some examples.

Form of Writing	Possible Purposes
Personal narrative	To entertain, to explain
Story	To entertain
Friendly letter	To entertain, to persuade, to explain, to inform
Business letter	To inform, to persuade
Instructions	To explain
Letter to the editor	To inform, to persuade
News article	To inform, to entertain, to explain

Writers may combine purposes in one form of writing. For example, an article about knitting might be both entertaining and informative.

Below is a list of written products. Write what you think the purpose of each item is—to entertain, persuade, explain, and/or inform.

Written Products

Purposes for Writing

a news article about a train wreck   _to inform, entertain, explain_

a personal narrative about a tragic incident   _to entertain, explain_

a story about a girl and her dog   _to entertain_

a business letter about a broken radio   _to inform, persuade_

Lesson 5 Audience

When a children's author sits down to write a story, does he write a 112-page book? Of course not. His audience would not be interested in such a long book. A children's author must think about his audience and write especially for them.

Does the president of a company have to think about her audience if she is writing a memo to her employees? They are adults; they can understand anything. Right? Wrong. If she is going to keep their interest and get her message across, she needs to think about her audience just as much as the children's author had to think about his.

Writers need to consider these questions every time they write.

- What will my audience enjoy?

- What are they interested in?

- What will make them want to keep on reading?

- What do they already know?

- What will they understand?

Mr. Elkins, the gym teacher, has to go to a meeting tomorrow. He has written a set of instructions for the substitute teacher. Mr. Elkins knows that the substitute teacher has never taught a gym class before. Read the paragraph. Think about whether Mr. Elkins kept his audience in mind.

After warm-ups, send the kids for two laps. Then, pick teams and have the fourth- and fifth-graders play dodge ball. The third-graders should play freeze tag. Set up all six centers for the first- and second-graders. Put the ball-bouncing center on the opposite side of the gym from the balancing center. Thanks and have a great day!

Lesson 5 Audience

Put yourself in Mr. Elkins' place and ask yourself the five questions on page 12. What else should Mr. Elkins have told the substitute teacher? Describe the sorts of things he should have included since he knew the substitute had never taught a gym class before.

_____

_____

_____

_____

Now, imagine that you are your own teacher. You also have a meeting tomorrow and must leave instructions for a substitute. What will the substitute need to make his or her way smoothly through the day? Remember, this substitute has never been in your classroom before. She knows the school's general schedule, but she doesn't know specific details about your class's schedule or about where things are in the room. Before you write your instructions here, ask yourself the five questions on page 12.

_____

_____

_____

_____

_____

_____

_____

_____

_____

_____

_____

_____

_____

_____

_____

_____

_____

Lesson 6 Write a Paragraph

Here is what you know about paragraphs.

> • A paragraph is a group of sentences that are all about the same topic.
>
> • Each sentence in a paragraph stays on topic.
>
> • The main idea of a paragraph is what the paragraph is all about.
>
> • A paragraph's main idea is usually stated in a topic sentence. The topic sentence may fall anywhere in the paragraph.
>
> • The first line of a paragraph is indented.
>
> • Writers must consider the audience for which they are writing.

What is your idea of a perfect summer day? What would the weather be like? What would you do? Where would you be? List some details that would be part of your perfect summer day.

Details:

_____   _____

_____   _____

_____   _____

Review your list. Think about the order in which you want to present your details in a paragraph. If you wish, number them. Then, draft a paragraph about your idea of a perfect summer day.

_____

_____

_____

_____

_____

_____

_____

_____

_____

_____

_____

Lesson 6 Write a Paragraph

Read through your paragraph. Ask yourself these questions. If necessary, make changes to your paragraph.

Questions to Ask About a Paragraph
Does the topic sentence express the main idea? **Does each sentence support the topic sentence?** **Does each sentence express a complete thought?** **Are the ideas and words in the paragraph appropriate for the audience?** **Is the first line indented?**

Now that you have thought about the content, or meaning, of your paragraph, proofread it for errors. Read through it several times, looking for a certain kind of error each time. Use this checklist.

____ spelling   ____ end marks

____ capitalization   ____ punctuation

Now, rewrite your paragraph. Use your neatest handwriting and make sure there are no errors in the final copy.

_____

_____

_____

_____

_____

_____

_____

_____

_____

_____

_____

_____

_____

_____

_____

_____

Chapter 2
Lesson 1 Personal Narrative

Have you ever written a true story about something that happened to you? You were writing a personal narrative. A personal narrative is a true story a writer tells about his or her own experiences. Read Jana's personal narrative.

Perfect Hindsight

After school, I delivered the note to Dad, went up to my room, shut the door, and burst into tears. The note was from Mrs. Schrum, the school nurse. I hadn't read the note, but I knew what it said.

It said that I had been able to see hardly anything during the vision screening. Everyone else had read at least four lines of letters on the chart. I could see the big **E** at the top, though it was a little fuzzy. Then, I guessed at the letters in the second row. I felt so stupid.

A little later, Dad came up to my room. Dad wears glasses, but that doesn't matter because he's a dad. He told me that he was only in fourth grade when he got his glasses. That was supposed to make me feel better because I'm in sixth grade. I just kept crying.

It was several weeks before Mom was able to get me to the eye doctor. I pretended that the doctor would say there had been some mistake. "This girl can see perfectly fine," he would announce.

In fact, the doctor just said, "Hmmm. Mm-hmm." Then, as if it were no surprise, he sent my parents and me to pick out frames. I tried on about a million of them. It was kind of fun, actually.

A week later, the glasses were ready. I guess I had gotten used to the idea. I was kind of eager. As soon as they were on, I said, "Hey, wow." I could read a sign all the way across the street! I had had no idea the glasses would make such a huge difference. Then, I grinned up at my parents. "This girl can see perfectly fine," I announced.

Lesson 1 Personal Narrative

Here are the features of a personal narrative:

- It tells a story about something that happens in a writer's life.
- It is written in the first person, using words such as *I, me, mine*, and *my*.
- It uses time and time-order words to tell events in a sequence.
- It expresses the writer's personal feelings.

Some people write personal narratives because they want to share their thoughts and feelings. Some write because they want to entertain their readers. Some might want to do both. As always, writers of personal narratives keep their audience in mind. What do they want to share with those readers that would be of interest? Finally, personal narratives can be about anything that actually happens to the writer.

What could you write a personal narrative about? Look at these idea-starters.

a beloved grandparent	a funny uncle	the first day at a new school
an athletic feat (or failure)	a family trip	an illness in the family
an embarrassing moment	getting braces	

What memories popped into your head as you read these idea-starters? Jot some notes about each memory or another one that you think of. One of these could be the start of a great personal narrative.

Idea-starter: _____

_____

_____

Idea-starter: _____

_____

_____

Idea-starter: _____

_____

_____

Lesson 2 Sequence of Events

In a personal narrative, readers need to know when things happen and in what order. Understanding the order of events helps readers put other ideas together, such as why something happened or what meaning an event had. Think of all the time-order words or phrases you can and list them. The list is started for you.

after school	next year	fourth grade
Tuesday	sunrise	last month

_____   _____   _____

_____   _____   _____

_____   _____   _____

_____   _____   _____

Now, use some of the time-order words from the list above. Write a sentence that could be from a personal narrative. Use a time-order word or phrase at the beginning of your sentence to tell when something happened.

_____

_____

_____

Write a sentence about something you did yesterday. Use a time-order word or phrase in the middle or at the end of your sentence.

_____

_____

_____

Lesson 2 Sequence of Events

In addition to time-order words, transition words help readers know when things happen and in what order. Here are some common transition words.

after	as soon as	before	during	finally	first
later	meanwhile	next	soon	then	when

Here is a paragraph from Jana's personal narrative on page 16. Circle the transition words when you find them.

A week later, the glasses were ready. I guess I had gotten used to the idea. I was kind of eager. As soon as they were on, I said, "Hey, wow." I could read a sign all the way across the street! I had had no idea the glasses would make such a huge difference. Then, I grinned up at my parents. "This girl can see perfectly fine," I announced.

Think about your morning routine. What do you do from the time you wake up until you get to school? Write this sequence of events in a paragraph. Remember that it is important to use transition and time-order words, but don't start every sentence with one. Use different sentence styles to keep your writing interesting.

_____

_____

_____

_____

_____

_____

_____

_____

_____

_____

_____

_____

_____

_____

_____

Lesson 3 Active Voice

Usually, the subject of a sentence does the action. That is easy to see in this sentence:

> Jason hung the picture.

The verb in the sentence is an active verb because the subject does the action.

What about this sentence?

> The picture was hung.

First, is this a complete sentence? Yes it is. It has a subject and a predicate. *Picture* is the subject of the sentence. Does the picture do the action? No, the picture does not do the action; the picture "receives" the action. The verb *was hung* is a passive verb because the subject does not do the action.

Passive verbs are always two-part verbs. There is always one of these helping *verbs—am, is, was, be, been*—plus a main verb. This does not mean that whenever you see one of those helping verbs, you are looking at a passive verb.

> Passive verb: Jason was called upstairs.

> Active verb: Jason was calling for help.

How can you tell the difference? Ask yourself these two questions:

> What is the subject?

> Is the subject doing the action?

If the answer to the second question is "yes," then you have an active verb. If the answer is "no," you have a passive verb.

Sometimes, you have to use passive verbs when you write. Maybe you don't know who did the action, so you have to write, "The picture was hung." Most of the time, however, our writing will be clearer and more interesting if you use active verbs.

Lesson 3 Active Voice

Compare these two paragraphs. The one on the left uses mostly passive verbs. The one on the right uses active verbs. What do you notice?

A grand opening was held last night by the art museum. A new exhibit was unveiled by the museum director. The collection of international textiles was assembled by Vince DiSilva. The textiles have been displayed previously by DiSilva in London and Los Angeles. The collection has been hailed by critics as the largest and most diverse of its kind.	The art museum held a grand opening last night. The museum director unveiled a new exhibit. Vince DiSilva assembled the collection of international textiles. DiSilva has displayed the textiles previously in London and Los Angeles. Critics have hailed the collection as the largest and most diverse of its kind.

Underline the subject of each sentence below. Put an **X** next to each sentence that contains a passive verb.

_____ Steve viewed the exhibit.

_____ The exhibit was lit with special lights.

_____ Elijah was looking at one display.

_____ Visitors were entertained by a pianist.

Practice writing sentences with active verbs. First, look at the sentences above that have passive verbs. Rewrite one of those sentences with an active verb.

_____

Now, write a new sentence about something that visitors might do at a museum. Make sure you use an active verb.

_____

Lesson 4 The Writing Process: Personal Narrative

Personal narratives can be about ordinary things. Remember the narrative you read on page 16? Jana wrote about getting glasses. Nothing dangerous or exciting happened. It was just an event in Jana's life, and it changed her a little bit. Follow the writing process to develop a personal narrative about an event in your own life. How did it change you?

Prewrite

Look again at the idea-starters on page 17 and the notes you made. Choose one of those ideas, or another idea that you like, and begin to explore it here.

My idea: _____

Use this idea web to collect and record details. Write down as many as you can.

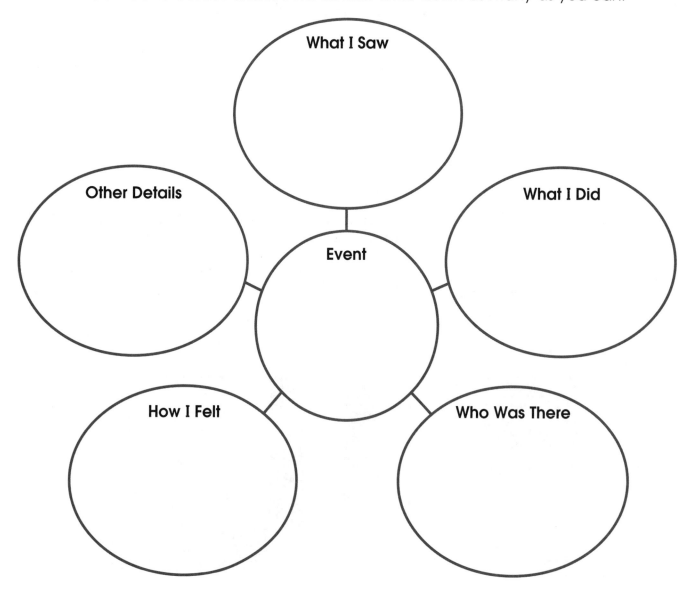

What I Saw

Other Details

What I Did

Event

How I Felt

Who Was There

Lesson 4 The Writing Process: Personal Narrative

So far, you have chosen a topic and collected ideas. Now it is time to put your ideas in order. Think about the "story" you are about to tell in your personal narrative. Use the sequence chart on this page to list the events in order. Don't worry about details here; just get the events down.

1. _____

2. _____

3. _____

4. _____

5. _____

6. _____

7. _____

8. _____

9. _____

Lesson 4 The Writing Process: Personal Narrative

Draft

Write the first draft of your personal narrative. Look back at your sequence chart on page 23 to keep yourself on track. Write your personal narrative on this page. Continue on another sheet of paper if you need to. As you write, don't worry about getting every word just right. Get your ideas down in sentences and in order.

_____

_____

_____

_____

_____

_____

_____

_____

_____

_____

_____

_____

_____

_____

_____

_____

_____

_____

_____

_____

_____

_____

Now that you have written your draft, write an idea for a title here.

Title: _____

Lesson 4 The Writing Process: Personal Narrative

Revise

One of the hardest things for any writer to do is to "fix" or change his or her own work. Writers put thought and effort into their work. It's hard not to read even a first draft and say, "Well, that's great." Good writers know that they can almost always improve their first drafts. Improve your own first draft by answering the questions below. If you answer "no" to any questions, those are the areas that might need improvement. Make notes on your draft about changes you might make later.

- Did you tell about just one event or one "thing" in your narrative?

- Did you include details to make readers feel as if they are right there with you?

- Did you tell events in order? Did you use transition and time-order words to show when events happened?

- Did you tell how you felt about the event? Do readers get a sense of your personal feelings?

- Did you use active verbs?

- Does your story flow smoothly when you read it out loud?

Now, focus on making sure you included details that will keep your readers interested. Did you use fantastic descriptive words, vivid verbs, and precise nouns?

When Jana revised her personal narrative, she replaced some overused verbs with more interesting ones. She also added the describing word *school* to help readers know what is happening. Here is how Jana changed the opening paragraph of her personal narrative.

After school, I ~~gave~~ delivered the note to Dad, went up to my room, shut the door, and ~~cried.~~ burst into tears The note was from Mrs. Schrum, the school nurse. I hadn't read the note, but I knew what it said.

Lesson 4 The Writing Process: Personal Narrative

Write the revision of your first draft. As you revise, remember to keep readers interested by using interesting words.

_____

_____

_____

_____

_____

_____

_____

_____

_____

_____

_____

_____

_____

_____

_____

_____

_____

_____

_____

_____

_____

_____

_____

_____

Now that you have revised your draft, are you still happy with your title? If not, write a new title here.

Title:_____

Lesson 4 The Writing Process: Personal Narrative

Proofread

Now is the time to correct those last errors. As you proofread, look for just one kind of error at a time. Read through once for capital letters, once for end punctuation, and once for spelling. Here is a checklist to help you proofread your revised narrative.

_____ Each sentence begins with a capital letter.

_____ Each sentence ends with the correct punctuation (period, question mark, or exclamation point).

_____ Each sentence states a complete thought.

_____ All words are spelled correctly. (If you're not sure, check a dictionary.)

When proofreaders work, they use certain symbols. Using these symbols makes their job easier. They will make your job easier, too.

Use these symbols as you proofread your personal narrative. Also, read your writing out loud. Sometimes, you hear mistakes that you don't see.

- Capitalize this letter.

- Add a missing end mark: ⊙ ? !

- Add a comma please.

- Fix incorrect or misspelled words.

- Delete this word.

- Lowercase this Letter.

Publish

Write a final copy of your personal narrative on a separate sheet of paper. If you wish, make a cover for it. You could even include photographs to go along with your narrative. Write carefully and neatly so that there are no mistakes.

Chapter 3

Lesson I Sensory Details

Scruunnch. I bit into my apple and juices flowed everywhere. At the same time, I felt some gooey brown caramel stick to my chin. I tried not to drool as I detached the bite of apple and got it all the way into my mouth. I had no napkin, wouldn't you know it, and had to fight the urge to wipe the sticky mess off on my white sleeve. I kept my head down so that no one would see the caramel hanging on my chin. I chewed quickly, though what I really wanted to do was savor the rich, sweet caramel blending with the tartness of the apple.

In a description, a writer's goal is to help readers see, hear, smell, feel, or taste what is being described. They use **sensory details**, or details that appeal to readers' senses, in their description. For example, in the paragraph above, *scruunnch* helps you hear the person biting the apple. The phrase "juices flowed everywhere" helps you feel what it's like to bite into the apple. What other sensory details does the paragraph contain? List them here, according to whether the detail helps you see, hear, smell, touch, or taste the caramel apple. Some details might fit into more than one category.

See: _____ _____ _____

Hear: _____ _____ _____

Smell: _____ _____ _____

Touch: _____ _____ _____

Taste: _____ _____ _____

Think about the last time you ate an apple. Was it covered in caramel? Maybe it was sliced up in a salad. How did it taste? What did it feel like? List the sensory details.

See: _____ _____ _____

Hear: _____ _____ _____

Smell: _____ _____ _____

Touch: _____ _____ _____

Taste: _____ _____ _____

NAME _____

Lesson I Sensory Details

Think of a food that you like. What is it like to eat that food? Imagine yourself eating and enjoying the food. Can you describe the experience so that a reader feels as if he or she is right there?

First, record the sights, sounds, smells, textures, and flavors you experience when you eat the food.

Sights: _____ _____ _____

Sounds: _____ _____ _____

Smells: _____ _____ _____

Textures: _____ _____ _____

Flavors: _____ _____ _____

Now, put your words to work. Describe what it is like to eat this food. Appeal to all five of your readers' senses. Remember to indent the first sentence of your paragraph.

_____
_____
_____
_____
_____
_____
_____
_____
_____
_____
_____
_____
_____
_____
_____
_____
_____
_____
_____

Lesson 2 Adjectives and Adverbs

To make a sentence, you need a noun and a verb. It takes just one of each to make a complete sentence.

Trucks rumble.

Adjectives and adverbs add description to a sentence.

- An **adjective** is a word that describes a noun or pronoun. Adjectives tell *what kind, how much* or *how many*, and *which ones*. In other words, adjectives tell how things look, sound, smell, feel, and taste.

- An **adverb** is a word that describes a verb, an adjective, or another adverb. Adverbs tell *how, when, where*, or *to what degree*. Many adverbs end in **ly**, but some do not, such as *not, never*, and *very*.

Adjectives at Work

Begin with a basic sentence and then notice how a few adjectives make it more interesting.

The trucks rumble down the street.

What kind of trucks are they? They are *huge* trucks.

How many trucks are there? There are *ten* of them.

What kind of street is it? It is a *bumpy* street.

Which trucks? It is *those* trucks.

Here is the new sentence. Notice that the adjectives go right before the nouns that they describe. This is almost always true. Doesn't this sentence make a more vivid image in your mind?

Those ten huge trucks rumble down the bumpy street.

Now, it is your turn. Look at the sentence below. Think of at least two adjectives to add to it, then write the new sentence. Remember, an adjective tells more about a noun or pronoun.

A driver blew his horn.

Lesson 2 Adjectives and Adverbs

Adverbs at Work

Start with the same basic sentence and see how some adverbs liven it up.

> The trucks rumble down the street.

When do the trucks rumble? They rumble *every day*.

How do they rumble? They rumble *noisily*.

Where do they rumble? They rumble *down the middle of the street*.

Here is the new sentence. Notice that one adverb comes several words before the verb it describes. The other falls right after the verb.

> Every day, the trucks rumble noisily down the middle of the street.

Look at each sentence below. Ask yourself whether you can add information about *how, when, where,* or *to what degree* with an adverb. Write your new sentence on the line.

A driver blows his horn.

_____

_____

The trucks roll to a stop at the corner.

_____

_____

Look at how both adjectives and adverbs work in this sentence.

    young   proudly   shiny, new
The driver stood next to his truck.

Improve each sentence by adding one adjective and one adverb to make the sentences more vivid.

The cab of a truck can be comfortable.

_____

_____

Trucks move goods across the country.

_____

_____

Lesson 3 Spatial Organization

When you walk into a room, you probably look around in an organized way. You might scan the room from left to right or from right to left. How you look at a room might depend on the size or shape of the room, what is in the room, or what is happening in the room.

When writers describe a room or some other place, they describe it in an organized way. This organization helps readers "see" the place just as if they were looking at it themselves. In the description of a skyscraper below, a writer describes the huge building from bottom to top.

> Just walking past on the sidewalk, you would never suspect anything. The doors were normal revolving glass doors. Through other windows, you could see people walking about in the lobby. But above the sidewalk, the building just kept going and going. Rows of windows blurred into one another. Beyond them, antennas and cell towers stretched even higher.

When organizing ideas by space, use words that tell where things are. Here are some common spatial words. Circle these, or other spatial words, in the paragraph above.

above	across	beside	between	beyond	into	left
low	middle	next to	over	right	through	under

Now, look at the room around you. Practice noticing details in an organized way. Write down what you see in the room. Use spatial words to describe where things are.

Left: _____

_____

Straight ahead: _____

_____

Right: _____

_____

Lesson 3 Spatial Organization

Imagine that you have climbed a mountain. At last, you are standing on the summit. What do you see? Describe the most distant detail first. Then, go on to describe what is in the middle distance, then what is nearest to you. Use sensory details so that readers can see, hear, smell, and feel the view. Also, remember to use spatial words to tell where things are.

_____

_____

_____

_____

_____

_____

_____

_____

_____

Imagine you are a member of a mountain climbing group. In your journal, you want to record the whole experience, so you describe the gear everyone is wearing. Organize the details of your description from top to bottom or from bottom to top.

_____

_____

_____

_____

_____

_____

_____

_____

_____

_____

_____

_____

Lesson 4 Describing Objects

When a writer describes an object, readers should be able to see, hear, smell, feel, and perhaps taste it. Can you describe something so vividly that your readers feel as if they are right there seeing it or holding it?

Take a close look at a shoe. Look at it as if you are seeing it for the first time. Record its details here.

Color: _____

Shape: _____

Size: _____

Texture: _____

Smell: _____

Other details: _____

Now, write a paragraph in which you describe the shoe. Again, describe it as if you are not familiar with the object. Remember to appeal to as many of your readers' senses as you can.

_____

_____

_____

_____

_____

_____

_____

_____

_____

_____

_____

_____

_____

_____

_____

_____

Lesson 4 Describing Objects

Now, try a more complex object, such as a backpack or book bag. Examine it. Even though it is a familiar object, look at it with fresh eyes. Record details of the object here.

Color: _____

Shape: _____

Size: _____

Texture: _____

Smell: _____

Other details: _____

Now, write a description of the object. Organize your details logically in a side-to-side or top-to-bottom format.

_____

_____

_____

_____

_____

_____

_____

_____

_____

_____

_____

_____

_____

_____

_____

_____

_____

_____

_____

_____

Lesson 5 The Language of Comparison

To compare two things, use the ending **-er** or the word *more* to talk and write about how the two things are different. These are **comparative** words and phrases.

> The first bear is *larger than* the second bear.
>
> The first bear is also *more monstrous than* the second bear.

For short words, such as *large*, add the **-er** ending. For longer words, such as *monstrous*, use *more* to compare.

Do some more comparing.

> Your snake is *fatter than* mine.
>
> My snake is *skinnier than* yours.

For some words, such as *red*, double the consonant, then add the **-er** ending. For words that end in **y**, change the **y** to **i**, then add **er**.

Note: *More* and the **-er** ending are never used at the same time. For example, it is not correct to write, "I ran more faster than you did."

Look at the pictures and compare them. Use comparative forms of the words given to complete each sentence below.

> One bed is _____ than the other. (lumpy)
>
> That bed must be _____ than the other. (uncomfortable)
>
> I would rather sleep on the _____ bed. (neat)

Write your own sentence about the beds. Use a comparative word or phrase. Remember to follow the spelling hints when you use **er** to to your comparing word.

_____

_____

Lesson 5 The Language of Comparison

When talking or writing about how three or more things are different, use the ending **-est** or the word *most*. These are **superlative** words and phrases.

The elephant is the *heaviest* of the three animals.

The dog has the *longest* fur.

The mouse has the *most delicate* feet.

The same spelling changes that occur when you add **er** to a word occur when you add **est** to a word. For example, *happiest* and *maddest* are correct spellings of superlative words.

Take your turn comparing three objects. Look at the pictures. Then, use the words *slow*, *speedy*, and *graceful* in sentences that compare the animals.

_____

_____

_____

_____

_____

_____

Errors in comparative and superlative words and phrases are common. Remember, use the ending **-er** or *most* when comparing two things. Use the ending **-est** or *most* when comparing three or more things. Can you find the errors in these comparisons? Write the correct comparative or superlative word or phrase on the line after each sentence.

Of my two dogs, Rex is the smartest. _____

Taylor is the taller of all the boys in the class. _____

That surprise birthday party was my most happiest moment. _____

Tara is the oldest of my two sisters. _____

Lesson 6 Comparing Objects

A Venn diagram is a tool that helps you compare things. In the diagram below, a dog and a cat are compared.

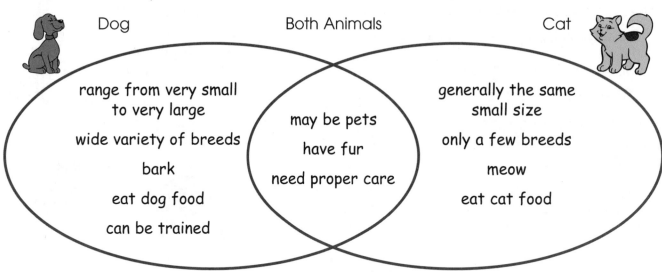

Dog   Both Animals   Cat

range from very small to very large

wide variety of breeds

bark

eat dog food

can be trained

may be pets

have fur

need proper care

generally the same small size

only a few breeds

meow

eat cat food

To practice using a Venn diagram, compare a regular balloon with a hot air balloon. Record how each item is different. Then, write what is the same about the two types of balloon.

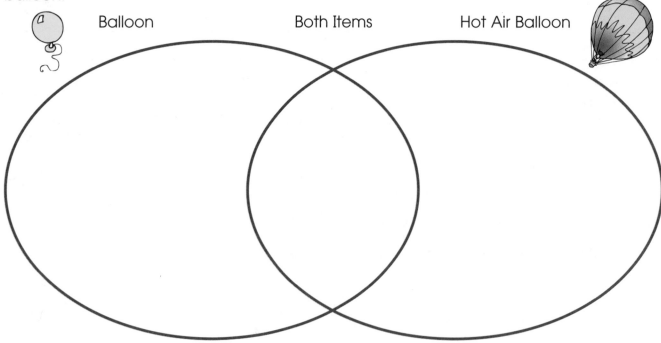

Balloon   Both Items   Hot Air Balloon

Once you organize ideas in a Venn diagram, you can more easily write about those ideas. When writers write to compare, they must present information in a way that makes sense to readers.

Lesson 6 Comparing Objects

There are two ways to organize a written comparison. One way is to talk first about one object, then about the other. This is called a **whole-to-whole comparison**. In this whole-to-whole comparison, information about an orange is in orange. Information about a lemon is in black.

This orange has a slightly bumpy, orange skin. When I peel the rind off, I can easily pull apart the sections. The taste is sweet. The lemon also has a slightly bumpy skin, but it is yellow. Inside, the sections are not quite so easy to pull apart. And it is the sourest thing I have ever put in my mouth.

The other way is to talk first about one feature, or characteristic, as it relates to both objects. Then, go on to another feature, and so on. This is a **part-to-part comparison**. Here is an example. Again, information about an orange is in orange; information about a lemon is in yellow.

This orange has a slightly bumpy, orange skin. The lemon also has a slightly bumpy skin, but it is yellow. When I peel the orange's rind off, I can easily pull apart the sections. Inside the lemon, the sections are not quite so easy to pull apart. The taste of the orange is sweet. The lemon is the sourest thing I have ever put in my mouth.

Now, look back at the details you recorded on page 38 about a balloon and a hot air balloon. Write a paragraph in which you compare the two items. Decide which method of organization you will use: whole-to-whole or part-to-part. Then, write the paragraph.

Organization: _____

_____

_____

_____

_____

_____

_____

_____

_____

_____

_____

Lesson 7 Comparing Characters

When you read, it is only natural to compare a book you are reading with other books you have read. You may note how situations or characters are alike or different. Comparing characters, whether within a book or among different books, can actually help you understand a story and its developments.

You already know how to compare things with the help of a Venn diagram. Emily made a diagram in her reader response journal to record what she knows so far about two characters in a book her class is reading.

Countdown by Ben Mikaelsen

| Elliot | Both Characters | Vincent |

in Montana

chosen as teenage astronaut

lives on ranch

dreamers

in conflict with fathers

in Kenya

Maasai

learns white men's ways from Sambeke

Think of characters in a book you are reading or have read lately. How are they alike and different? Fill out this Venn diagram with what you know about the characters. Think about how the characters act, or how they respond to what happens to them. Remember to label the circles with the characters' names.

_____

_____   Both Characters   _____

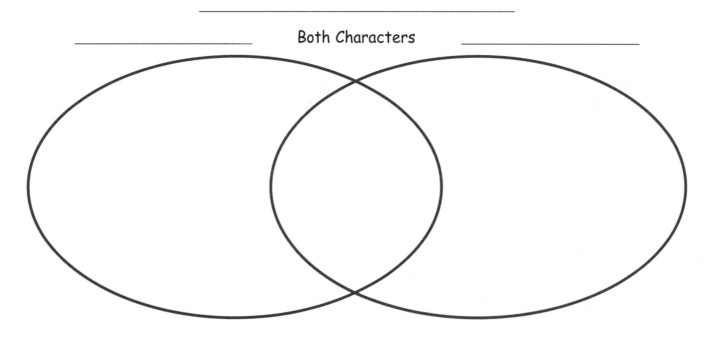

Lesson 7 Comparing Characters

Emily's teacher has asked the students to write about Elliot and Vincent, the characters from the book. Emily reviews her Venn diagram, then chooses whole-to-whole organization for her paragraph. In other words, she'll talk first about one boy, then the other.

Elliot is a 14-year-old boy who has a lot of responsibility. His dad depends on him to help take care of the cattle on the family's ranch. Elliot rides his beloved horse everywhere, fixing fences and rescuing cattle as needed. He also longs to go to space, and NASA has accepted him as a teenage astronaut. Elliot's father doesn't fully understand Elliot's dreams and doesn't want him to leave the ranch.

Vincent is also 14 years old and also takes care of cattle. His family are Maasai herders in Kenya. Like Elliot, he is responsible for the cattle. He takes them out to graze each day and protects them from lions and other dangers. Vincent has a friend, Sambeke, who teaches him about white men's ways. Vincent's father does not approve and does not want Vincent to spend any time with Sambeke.

Now, review your own Venn diagram on page 40 and write about your two characters. Decide whether you will use whole-to-whole organization, as Emily did, or part-to-part. Look back on pages 38 and 39 to review the two methods if you wish.

_____

_____

_____

_____

_____

_____

_____

_____

_____

_____

_____

_____

_____

_____

_____

_____

Lesson 8 The Writing Process: Descriptive Writing

Descriptive writing plays a role in many forms of writing. You see it in stories, in textbooks, and in newspaper articles. You can use the writing process to develop a paragraph that describes a setting of a story.

Prewrite

Suppose you are trying to describe a place to someone who has never seen it. It could be a hidden cave, a hideout in a tree, or even a space station. First, think of some places that you could describe thoroughly. List them here.

Places I could describe:

_____   _____

_____   _____

_____   _____

Now, look over your list. Which place do you think you can describe most vividly? Choose one and write the place that you decide on here.

Place I will describe: _____

Use this idea web to collect and record details about your place.

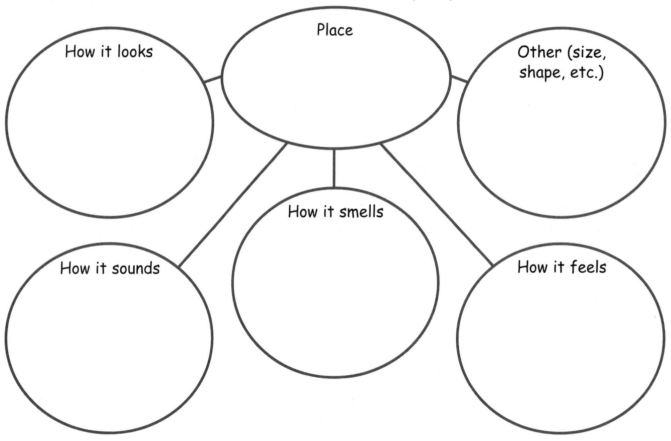

Lesson 8 The Writing Process: Descriptive Writing

As a final step in the prewriting stage, organize your ideas. How will you describe this place—from top to bottom? From side to side? Make a choice and record it here.

Method of organization: _____

Major details, in order:

Draft

Refer to your prewriting notes as you write a first draft. Remember, this is the time to get your ideas down on paper in sentences. This is not the time to worry about getting every word just right.

_____

_____

_____

_____

_____

_____

_____

_____

_____

_____

_____

_____

Lesson 8 The Writing Process: Descriptive Writing

Revise

All writers face the difficult task of reading what they have just written and trying to make it better. Reread your draft carefully. Will it be clear to your readers? Answer the questions, below, about your draft. If you answer "no" to any of these questions, then those areas might need improvement.

- Did you keep your audience in mind? Did you include details that will interest them and that they will understand?

- Did you organize your description in a logical, spatial way?

- Did you use spatial words to show where things are?

- Did you use vivid verbs and precise nouns to help readers see the place?

- Did you use sensory details? To how many of your readers' senses did you appeal?

Rewrite your description here. Make changes to improve your message based on the questions you just answered.

_____

_____

_____

_____

_____

_____

_____

_____

_____

_____

_____

_____

_____

_____

_____

Lesson 8 The Writing Process: Descriptive Writing

Proofread

Your description should be in good shape now. The last task is to check it for any remaining errors. It is best to read for one kind of error at a time. Proofread your revision on page 44. Use this checklist to help you catch all of the errors.

____ Does each sentence begin with a capital letter?

____ Does each sentence have an appropriate end mark?

____ Are proper nouns (names of people, places, or things) capitalized?

____ Are all words spelled correctly?

Publish

Write a final copy of your description here. Use your best handwriting. Be careful not to introduce any new errors.

_____

_____

_____

_____

_____

_____

_____

_____

_____

_____

_____

_____

_____

_____

_____

_____

_____

_____

Chapter 4

Lesson 1 Parts of a Story

A good story has these ingredients:

- A story tells about made-up people or animals. They are the **characters** in the story.

- A story has a **setting** where the action takes place.

- A story's action is the **plot**. The plot is usually a series of events that includes a **conflict**, or problem, which needs to be solved.

- A story uses **dialogue**, or conversation among the characters, to move the action of the story along.

- An interesting **beginning**, **middle**, and **end** make a story fun to read.

- **Describing words** tell about the characters, setting, and events.

Read the first part of a science fiction story below. Then, answer the questions that follow.

The Colony

Even after 472 days, I hadn't gotten used to the quietness of this place. I was walking on hard ground, yet my footfalls hardly made a sound. In the distance, I could see the colony's generator. I knew it was churning and making noise, but I couldn't hear it at all. On Earth, I would have said that quietness was peaceful. Up here, though, the quiet just seemed empty.

An hour passed, and I was pleased at my progress. My distance meter showed that I was more than half way. No one from the colony had walked as far as Monroe Flats before, and I wasn't exactly sure of what I would find along the way. I liked walking, but I hoped I wouldn't have to detour around any craters. I had plenty to do. As the colony's Environment Manager, I made daily tests on soil and atmosphere. They were vital to the colony's success.

With my head down, I worked my way up a slope when I saw something in the gray, dusty sand. I staggered backward, like a person who shies away from a snake. There was a track on the dusty hillside. I felt a sudden plunge in my stomach. *No one's been out here!* I thought. I looked to the left. The track continued about 40 meters, then wound around the curve of the slope. To the right, it went downward, to the base of the slope, and out of sight.

The track was just a sort of a swishy trail, as if someone had walked along dragging a heavy sack right behind, so that his or her footprints were covered. *Why would someone from the colony have been dragging something out here?* My mind was racing. *Surely I would have known.* Anyway, most people used transport modules when they were away from the colony. I kept looking left and right, as if I were checking for traffic. I jumped when my Telewave beeped.

"Morgan? Are you there?"

I spoke into the device on my wrist. "Yes, Chairman." The chairman would know who else was out here.

Lesson 1 Parts of a Story

"Those supplies you ordered just arrived," the Chairman's voice said in its usual smooth tones.

"Oh," I waited, expecting more information. When it didn't come, I added, "Thank you, sir,"

"Alright. See you tonight, Morgan."

"Yes, sir....Sir?" There was no response. The buzzing on my Telewave told me that there would be no further communication. Atmospheric disturbances often interrupted off-site transmissions.

I stood there feeling stupid because I couldn't decide what to do. I studied the track again to see if I could determine in which direction the person had been traveling. I noticed a pattern in the sand that seemed to indicate that the person had come from the bottom of the slope up to this point. I squinted up to the left. Nothing. Without really even deciding, I went in that direction.

Lesson 1 Parts of a Story

Answer these questions about "The Colony." Look back at the story on pages 46 and 47 if you need to.

Who is the main character in the story? _____

List three details about the main character.

_____   _____   _____

What other character appears in the story? _____

What do you know about this character?

_____

Where does the action take place? _____

What details does the writer reveal about the place? List some here.

_____   _____

_____   _____

What main problem occurs? _____

How does the main character deal with the problem at this point?

_____

Review the dialogue. Notice what the characters say and how they say it. What do you learn about the characters from the dialogue?

Main character: _____

_____

Other character: _____

_____

Record some of the story's sensory details. Remember to look for sights, sounds, smells, textures, and tastes.

_____   _____   _____

_____   _____   _____

_____   _____   _____

Lesson 2 Setting

Every story has to take place somewhere. The setting of a story is when and where the action takes place. The setting of a story may be in a real place or in a completely imagined place. The time during which a story takes place may be in the past, the present, or the future.

In some stories, readers learn details of the setting almost by accident. Perhaps a character complains about the "rotten weather," so you can assume it is cold or rainy. Maybe you learn from a character's thoughts that he is tired of sitting in the doctor's waiting room. In other stories, the narrator describes the setting. Here is an example from "A Mystery of Heroism," by Stephen Crane.

> Sometimes they of the infantry looked down at a fair little meadow which spread at their feet. Its long, green grass was rippling gently in a breeze. Beyond it was the grey form of a house half torn to pieces by shells and by the busy axes of soldiers who had pursued firewood. The line of an old fence was now dimly marked by long weeds and by an occasional post. A shell had blown the well-house to fragments. Little lines of grey smoke ribboning upward from some embers indicated the place where had stood the barn.

Look at all the information in that paragraph:

The characters—"they of the infantry"—are on a hill, because they "looked down" at the meadow. It is spring or summer; the grass is long and green. In contrast to the pleasant meadow are the remains of a battle. A house in the distance is standing in ruins, and a well-house and a barn are destroyed.

Now, think of a story or book that you have read. What do you remember about the setting? Remember to think about the time (such as the year), the weather, the time of day, and physical location in all of its details. Write what you remember.

Title: _____

Setting: _____

_____

_____

_____

_____

_____

_____

_____

_____

Lesson 2 Setting

Here is another example. The setting is described by the main character, who is also the narrator. This passage is from "The Colony," the science-fiction story you read on pages 46 and 47.

> Even after 472 days, I hadn't gotten used to the quietness of this place. I was walking on hard ground, yet my footfalls hardly made a sound. In the distance, I could see the colony's generator. I knew it was churning and making noise, but I couldn't hear it at all. On Earth, I would have said that quietness was peaceful. Up here, though, the quiet just seemed empty.

What information do you get about the setting from this passage?

_____

_____

_____

What mood, or feeling, do you get from the passage?

_____

What words or details convey that mood?

_____

Writers use details in their settings that match the mood of what is happening in the story. First, think about details that a writer might include in a story that is humorous or light-hearted.

What might the weather be like?

_____

What time of day might it be?

_____

Now, think about setting details that a writer might include in a scary part of a story, or in a part where something bad is going to happen to a character.

What might the weather be like?

_____

What time of day might it be?

_____

Lesson 2 Setting

Look over the details you recorded for "light-hearted" settings and "scary" or "bad" settings. Are you starting to imagine a great story? Choose one of the settings you've already begun to visualize and develop it further here.

Write a few paragraphs that describe the setting. Indicate both when and where the action takes place. Remember to organize your details in a way that makes sense. For example, if you are describing a distant view, you might go from left to right or from far to near. Think about which method makes most sense for your setting.

_____

_____

_____

_____

_____

_____

_____

_____

_____

_____

_____

_____

_____

_____

_____

_____

_____

_____

_____

_____

_____

_____

_____

Lesson 3 Characters

Some stories have terrific characters. Can you remember cheering for them when something good happened? Did you hope that the character's bad times would turn out alright? Name some memorable characters you remember from stories or novels you have read.

_____   _____

_____   _____

Now, think about what you know about those characters. How did you learn about them? How did the narrator or author help you get to know the character? Normally, readers learn about characters in four ways:

- The narrator reveals information.

- The character's own words reveal information.

- The character's actions reveal information.

- Other characters' words and actions reveal information.

Review "The Colony" on pages 46 and 47. What do you know about the main character? For each detail you record, write how you know it. For example, from the first sentence you learn that he has been somewhere for 472 days. You know this because the narrator (who is also the main character) reveals that information.

What I Know About the Character   **How I Know It**

_____   _____

_____   _____

_____   _____

_____   _____

_____   _____

_____   _____

_____   _____

_____   _____

_____   _____

_____   _____

_____   _____

Lesson 3 Characters

Now, think about a character you would like to create. Rather than thinking about what happens to the character, think about what kind of person the character is. Answer these questions.

Is the character human? _____ If not, what is the character? _____

Is the character male or female? _____

What two words best describe your character?

_____   _____

What does your character look like? Is he or she carrying something?

_____

What might your character say? How might your character say it? Write a line of dialogue that your character might speak.

_____

What might other characters say about this character? Either write some dialogue or describe what others would say.

_____

_____

_____

_____

Now, introduce your character. Write a paragraph about him or her.

_____

_____

_____

_____

_____

_____

_____

_____

_____

_____

_____

_____

Lesson 4 Dialogue

Dialogue is the conversation among characters in a story. Good dialogue helps readers get to know the characters. It also keeps the action of the story moving. Here is what dialogue looks like.

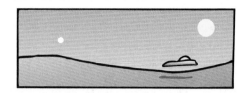

> The Chairman looked thoughtfully out the window. "Morgan seemed a little distracted," he said. "I hope he's alright."
>
> Smiling, Kip replied, "Oh, I'm sure he is, sir."
>
> "How far did he say he was going?" asked the Chairman.
>
> Kip checked a chart. "To Monroe Flats, sir."
>
> "Monroe Flats!" burst the Chairman. "He's walking?"
>
> "Yes, sir," said Kip, a little surprised at the Chairman's outburst. "He likes to walk," Kip added, thinking it might calm his boss. It didn't.
>
> "Is he mad?" ranted the Chairman. "No one knows what's out there. Send a patrol in a transport module to get him. Right away."

What do you learn about the Chairman from this dialogue?

_____

What do you learn about Kip?

_____

Take a closer look at a line of dialogue and its punctuation.

| The **tag line** tells who is speaking. | **Quotation marks** go before and after the speaker's exact words. |

Smiling, Kip replied, "Oh, I'm sure he is, sir."

| A **comma** separates the tag line from the speaker's words. | **End punctuation** goes inside the quotation marks. If a sentence ends in a period and the tag line comes after the quotation, change the period to a comma. |

The speaker's first word begins with a capital letter, even if that word is not the first word of the sentence.

Lesson 4 Dialogue

Below is some dialogue that has not been punctuated. Add the punctuation. Look at the dialogue on page 54 for examples if you need to. Pay close attention to the position of commas and end marks.

I wonder why the Chairman is so upset said Kip

The Chairman yelled Morgan should never have gone that far out

Is the transport module ready yet he asked

Dialogue should sound like real people talking. An 11-year-old character should sound more or less like you sound. An adult should sound like an adult. Remember, however, that people sound different from each other. People have different speech patterns based on where they grew up, what education they've had, and where they live.

Write a conversation between yourself and the Chairman, the leader of the space colony in the story on pages 46 and 47. Make the dialogue sound realistic. Stop and think how you would speak to a person who is in charge. How would he speak to you? Remember to use quotation marks and tag lines. Look at the examples on page 54 if you need to. The dialogue is started for you.

"Sir, I received your Telewave message. Why did you ask me to bring a transport module?" I asked.

_____

_____

_____

_____

_____

_____

_____

_____

_____

_____

_____

_____

_____

Lesson 5 Point of View

When a writer writes a story, he or she chooses a narrator to tell the story. In some stories, the narrator is one of the characters in the story. Words such as *I, me*, and *my* let readers know that this is happening. This is called **first-person point of view**. Here is another piece of "The Colony," the story begun on pages 46 and 47.

As I followed the track, I realized that I was tight all over. My toes, fingers, and even my teeth were clenched. I jogged a few steps and shook my arms out. In training, they had always told you to stay relaxed. If you were tense, you couldn't respond as quickly. *Respond to what?* I thought. *Who in the world could be out here?*

I suppose the jogging and unclenching distracted me. It wasn't until I was fully at the top of the hill that I saw the crater and what was in it. I automatically held my Telewave up to my mouth.

"Jasper Colony, this is Morgan. Get me the Chairman," I said. A crackle assured me that my call was being transmitted. Then, the abrupt bark of the Chairman's voice made me jump.

"Morgan, what are you doing out there?" the Chairman asked.

Here is the same scene, but it is written in **third-person point of view**. Readers see words such as *he, she, him, her, his, they*, and *them* in stories that are written in third person. The narrator is not a character in the story. The main character is the same, but the **omniscient**, or all-knowing, narrator "reports" to readers what the character says, thinks, and does.

As he followed the track, Morgan realized that he was tight all over. His toes, fingers, and even his teeth were clenched. He jogged a few steps and shook his arms out. In training, they had always told him to stay relaxed. If he were tense, he couldn't respond as quickly. *Respond to what?* he thought. *Who in the world could be out here?*

He supposed the jogging and the unclenching distracted him. It wasn't until he was fully at the top of the hill that he saw the crater and what was in it. He automatically held his Telewave up to his mouth.

"Jasper Colony, this is Morgan. Get me the Chairman," he said. A crackle assured him that his call was being transmitted. Then, the abrupt bark of the Chairman's voice made him jump.

"Morgan, what are you doing out there?" the Chairman asked. He felt that things were beginning to get out of hand.

Lesson 5 Point of View

Look back at the piece of the story on page 56. What do you think is in the crater? What happens next? Write the next paragraph in first-person point of view. Remember, in first person the narrator is a character in the story. Readers learn what he or she is thinking and feeling. The narrator does not know what other characters are thinking and feeling.

_____

_____

_____

_____

_____

_____

_____

_____

_____

Now, write that same scene in third-person point of view. Remember, Morgan is still the main character. The all-knowing narrator is not a character, but will tell what Morgan says, thinks, and does. The narrator will also tell what any other character says, thinks, and does.

_____

_____

_____

_____

_____

_____

_____

_____

_____

_____

Lesson 6 Story Ideas

Many stories that you read are **realistic**. They include characters who are more or less normal. Realistic stories set in the past are called *historical fiction*. Whether the setting is in the past or the present, though, the characters could be real, and the events could happen, even though the details come from a writer's imagination.

List some stories or books you have read that have realistic settings. Briefly describe the settings.

Title   **Setting**

_____   _____

_____   _____

_____   _____

_____   _____

What kind of realistic story would you like to write? Will it be about an adventure that a kid had while he lived on the frontier in a log cabin? Will it be about a modern-day kid who is a computer genius? Realistic stories require just as much imagination as unrealistic, or fantasy, stories do. Write down some realistic story ideas.

Realistic story idea #1

Character(s): _____

Setting:_____

Plot:_____

_____

Realistic story idea #2

Character(s): _____

Setting:_____

Plot:_____

_____

Lesson 6 Story Ideas

Fiction that is set in the future is usually called *science fiction*. The setting may be on Earth or in another world of some sort. Characters may be human or some other life form. Details often involve advanced, or futuristic, technology that the author imagines.

What science fiction stories have you read? Try to recall some of the details. For example, were the characters human? Where did the characters live? Did the author reveal the year? Record a few details that you remember.

_____

_____

What kind of science fiction would you like to write? Who will be your main characters? Where will they live? Why are they there? What year is it? Open up your imagination and jot down a couple of science fiction ideas here.

Science fiction idea #1

Character(s): _____

Setting:_____

Plot:_____

_____

Science fiction idea #2

Character(s): _____

Setting:_____

Plot:_____

_____

Lesson 7 The Writing Process: Story

Some writers use their surroundings to help them create a character, setting, or plot for a story. Perhaps they base a character's home on a house they used to live in. Maybe a character's grandfather is much like the writer's grandfather. Other writers create whole new worlds. They imagine life in the future in ways that seem completely fantastic to readers. Use the writing process and see what kind of world you can create for a story.

Prewrite

Look at the story ideas you sketched out on pages 58 and 59. Choose one of those ideas or another idea that you like and begin to develop it. Whether you write a realistic story or science fiction, you need to pay special attention to your main character. Use this idea web to record details about how he or she looks, acts, speaks, and so on.

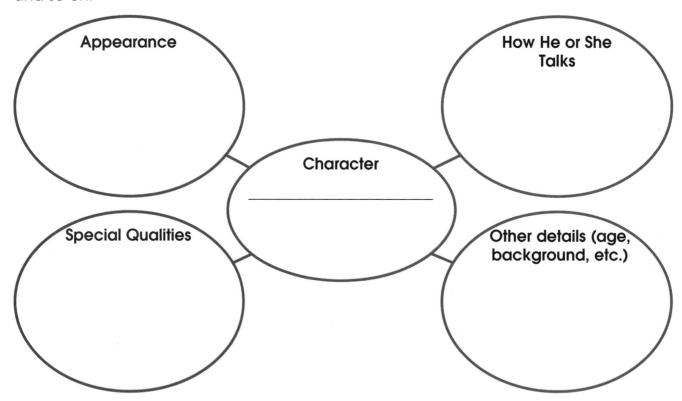

Before you continue, consider these questions about your setting and plot.

- What is the setting of your story? Consider place or location, time setting (year), season, time of day, weather, and so on.

- What problem will the character face?

- What does the character do to try to solve the problem? Does it take more than one try? What is the final solution or outcome?

Lesson 7 The Writing Process: Story

Now, put the main events of your story together. Think about the story you are about to tell. What is at the beginning, in the middle, and at the end? Use the story map on this page to plan the important parts of your story.

Character(s)
_____

Setting
_____

Plot: Beginning
_____
_____
_____
_____

Plot: Middle
_____
_____
_____
_____
_____
_____
_____

Plot: End
_____
_____
_____
_____

Lesson 7 The Writing Process: Story

Draft

Write a first draft of your story. Refer to your story map as you write the draft. Continue on another sheet of paper if you need to. As you write, don't worry about mistakes. Just get your ideas down in sentences and in order.

_____

_____

_____

_____

_____

_____

_____

_____

_____

_____

_____

_____

_____

_____

_____

_____

_____

_____

_____

_____

_____

_____

Write some ideas for a title here. You may choose the final title later.

Title:_____

Lesson 7 The Writing Process: Story

Revise

Every writer must look at his or her work with fresh eyes and figure out how to make the writing better. Even experienced writers do this, and no one considers it an easy job.

Answer the questions below. If you answer "no" to any of these questions, those are the areas you might need to improve. Make marks on your draft so you know what needs attention.

> * Did you give details about an interesting character and a setting?
>
> * Does your story have a beginning, a middle, and an end?
>
> * Did you include a problem and a solution in your plot?
>
> * Did you tell events in an order that made sense?
>
> * Did you use sensory details?
>
> * Did you use dialogue to help readers learn about characters and to move the story forward?

Review the important parts of a story.

* In the **beginning** of a story, readers meet the character or characters and learn a little about the setting and the plot. The first sentence makes readers want to keep on reading.

* In the **middle** of a story, the action takes place. Readers see the character or characters face a problem. The characters probably make one or more attempts to solve the problem.

* In the **end**, the characters solve the problem in a logical way. Keep in mind that it is not satisfying to have a story's central problem just go away by magic or by coincidence. Your characters must deal with or solve their problem.

On your draft, draw brackets next to the beginning, middle, and end of your story. Jot some notes if you decide that you must revise any of those parts to make them more interesting for your readers.

Lesson 7 The Writing Process: Story

Read your draft out loud. Listen for awkward sentences or sentences that sound too much the same. Then, write the revision of your story here. Fix those awkward sentences as you go.

_____

_____

_____

_____

_____

_____

_____

_____

_____

_____

_____

_____

_____

_____

_____

_____

_____

_____

_____

_____

_____

_____

_____

Review your title choices. Which one seems best? Write it here.

Title:_____

Lesson 7 The Writing Process: Story

Proofread

By now, you have read your story several times. You can probably recite parts from memory. It is still important, though, to proofread carefully. When you are familiar with what you are reading, you are more likely to overlook errors. Also, you must still proofread typewritten text, even if the computer has checked your spelling. If you type *form* instead of *from*, for example, the computer won't catch that error. Use the checklist below as you proofread your revised story. Read for one kind of error at a time.

____ Each sentence begins with a capital letter.

____ Each sentence ends with the correct punctuation (period, question mark, or exclamation point).

____ Dialogue is punctuated correctly.

____ Each sentence states a complete thought.

____ All words are spelled correctly.

When proofreaders work, they use certain symbols. Using these symbols will make your job easier.

Use these symbols as you proofread your story. Remember to read your writing out loud to yourself. When you read out loud, you may hear mistakes or rough spots that you did not see.

- $\underline{\underline{c}}$apitalize this letter.

- Add a missing end mark: $\odot$? !

- Add a comma$_\wedge$please.

- "Be sure to punctuate your dialogue,$^{\prime\prime}$she said.

- Fix incor$\overset{r}{\wedge}$ect or misspelled words.

- ~~Delete~~ this word.

- Lowercase this $\cancel{L}$etter.

Publish

Write a final copy of your story on a separate sheet of paper. Write or type carefully so that there are no mistakes. If you wish, add illustrations and make a cover or title page. Share your story with friends and family.

Chapter 5

Lesson 1 Persuasive Writing

You see persuasive writing every day. You may not even be aware of it. A bus passes by with a sign on its side. In your favorite magazine, you read the letters to the editor. In the school newspaper, a fellow student has written an article about the proposed changes in class offerings for next year. Whatever the form that persuasive writing takes, the writer's goal is to try to make readers think, feel, or act in a certain way.

Here is an example of a persuasive article. The writer gives some information and states her opinion. She closes with a statement that requests some of her readers to take action.

> ## New Classes: Change for the Better?
>
> Times are changing. At least, that's what next year's class list seems to indicate. As of next fall, some classes will never again be offered at OMS.
>
> The home economics department will see drastic changes. Traditional cooking classes are a thing of the past. Instead, students will take a class called *consumer science*. The former home economics rooms will house three new computer labs plus a video lab. Proposed class offerings involve creating multimedia presentations, manipulating digital images, conducting online research, and more.
>
> My question is this: Don't we need to learn how to cook any more? Maybe it's old-fashioned, but everyone needs to eat. With parents working full-time jobs these days, they have less time to teach us those skills. I like the idea of the new computer offerings, but I don't believe it was the best idea to do away with the basics. Unless people want to rely on fast-food restaurants or convenience foods, cooking is pretty important, I think. I hope the school administrators will reconsider the plan and continue to offer cooking classes.
>
> By Mariah Wayne

It is a good idea to be aware of persuasive writing. For a few days, keep track of the things you see that include persuasive writing. Record them here.

_____   _____

_____   _____

_____   _____

_____   _____

_____   _____

_____   _____

_____   _____

_____   _____

Lesson 1 Persuasive Writing

Do you think it's important to have a cooking class in middle school? Do you think those skills are no longer necessary? Respond to Mariah's article on page 66. State your opinion and support it with reasons. Assume that your article will appear in the school newspaper. Make sure that your opinion is clear and that readers understand what you want them to think or do. How persuasive can you be?

_____

_____

_____

_____

_____

_____

_____

_____

_____

_____

_____

_____

_____

_____

_____

_____

_____

_____

_____

_____

_____

_____

_____

_____

_____

_____

Lesson 2 Facts and Opinions

Which of these sentences below is a fact? Which is an opinion? If you're not sure, ask yourself these questions: Which statement could be proven true? That would be a **fact**. Which is a belief or a personal judgment? That would be an **opinion**.

Cooking classes are no longer offered in many schools.

Cooking classes are a vital part of a middle school education.

Often, writers state both facts and opinions. That is okay, but writers and readers both must be able to tell the difference between the two. Look for facts and opinions as you reread Mariah's article.

New Classes: Change for the Better?

Times are changing. At least, that's what next year's class list seems to indicate. As of next fall, some classes will never again be offered at OMS.

The home economics department will see drastic changes. Traditional cooking classes are a thing of the past. Instead, students will take a class called *consumer science*. The former home economics rooms will house three new computer labs plus a video lab. Proposed class offerings involve creating multimedia presentations, manipulating digital images, conducting online research, and more.

My question is this: Don't we need to learn how to cook any more? Maybe it's old-fashioned, but everyone needs to eat. With parents working full-time jobs these days, they have less time to teach us those skills. I like the idea of the new computer offerings, but I don't believe it was the best idea to do away with the basics. Unless people want to rely on fast-food restaurants or convenience foods, cooking is pretty important, I think. I hope the school administrators will reconsider the plan and continue to offer cooking classes.

By Mariah Wayne

Using the persuasive writings you found and recorded on page 66, explain why they are persuasive.

_____

_____

_____

_____

_____

_____

_____

_____

Lesson 2 Facts and Opinions

Words such as *think, believe, should, must, never, always, like, hate, best,* and *worst* may signal that a statement is an opinion. Scan the article again and circle any opinion signal words you find,

Write two facts from the article.

_____

_____

Write two opinions from the article.

_____

_____

One of Mariah's classmates has written her own opinion about the new classes at OMS. Read Tisha's paragraph and look for opinion signal words.

> I think it's about time this school got into the 21st century. At last, we have some decent computer classes. The old cooking classes were always useless. Who can't microwave a frozen waffle? The new classes will teach us to create and use digital images in all sorts of ways. That is a much more useful skill than cooking. I look forward to the new classes and believe that everyone will be better off.

Write one fact from Tisha's paragraph.

_____

_____

Circle any opinion signal words that you find in Tisha's paragraph. Then, write one opinion that Tisha states.

_____

_____

Now, state your own opinion about cooking class versus computer classes. Which do you think is more valuable?

_____

_____

_____

_____

Lesson 3 Emotional Appeals

How do writers get readers to think, feel, or act in a certain way when they write persuasively? Often, they appeal to readers' emotions. When writers make an **emotional appeal**, they try to get at something about which readers feel strongly. For example, Ms. Martinez, the home economics teacher, thinks cooking classes are important. She included this statement in a letter to the editor:

> Our job is to prepare students for life beyond school. Computers and computer classes are available to students in many ways. Cooking classes, however, are available to students only while they are in middle school. If we don't offer cooking classes, we are not doing our jobs.
>
> Ms. Martinez

Ms. Martinez knows that most people feel strongly about doing their jobs well. She also knows that many people feel strongly about education and about their local schools. Though the statements are opinions (rather than facts), they have a strong emotional appeal and may persuade some readers to believe as the writer does.

Many people have strong feelings about positive issues such as these:

justice	family	security	education
money	home	safety	conservation

People may also have strong feelings toward negative issues such as these:

injustice	crime	waste
violence	pollution	danger

Name some issues about which you have strong feelings.

_____   _____   _____

_____   _____   _____

_____   _____   _____

Emotional appeals may tie into readers' strong feelings about positive or negative issues. Read the letter to the editor on the next page. What kind of emotional appeal does the writer make?

Lesson 3 Emotional Appeals

Dear Editor:

In Lora Webb's article (May 23) about the middle school, she mentions that woodworking class will no longer be offered. I took that class in 1988. My teacher, Mr. Harker, taught me it was okay that I wasn't an "A" student. He also taught me valuable skills, such as planning ahead and sticking with a job until it's done. During high school, I got a part-time job in a furniture factory. I almost dropped out of high school, but I knew my boss would fire me if I quit school. So I stuck with it. After high school, I got a full-time job at another factory. I improved my skills and am now able to work for myself as a cabinetmaker. Without the skills I learned from Mr. Harker in woodworking class, I'm pretty sure I would have become a high school dropout. I know that computers are important in my business, but I wonder if those new computer classes will teach kids any skills that are half as valuable as the ones I learned in woodworking class.

N. Scariffe, Andersonville

Explain the emotional appeal in Mr. Scariffe's letter to the editor.

_____

_____

_____

_____

Write a letter to the editor in response to Mr. Scariffe's letter. Write in support of his opinion or indicate why you disagree with him. Remember to consider your audience. What kind of emotional appeal might make people agree with you?

Dear Editor:

_____

_____

_____

_____

_____

_____

_____

_____

_____

_____

_____

_____

_____

_____

_____

_____

Lesson 4 Advertising

Ready Printing Co.

**Reliable.
On time.
Comfortable.**

If you are a very persuasive writer, you might consider a job writing advertisements. Advertising copywriters rely heavily on emotional appeals to win over customers. They know that people have strong feelings about wanting to feel good, to fit in, and to have fun. Advertisements constantly send messages that writers think people want to hear.

Look at the Ready Printing Co. logo. What does the word *comfortable* have to do with using a printing company?

_____

_____

What message does the drinking water slogan send?

_____

_____

Advertising copywriters know that thinking about audience is especially important. Perhaps the most often-asked questions are these: Who might buy this product? What kind of advertising message can persuade them to buy?

Suppose you are writing an advertisement for child's car seat. Who is your audience?

_____

_____

To which strong feelings do you need to appeal to get this audience to buy your car seats?

_____

_____

Lesson 4 Advertising

Imagine you are an advertising copywriter. Think up a slogan for a new fast-food restaurant that offers only soups and salads. First, think about who the audience is. About what kinds of issues might they have strong feelings? In your slogan, make an emotional appeal.

[ ]

Now, your next assignment is to create a slogan for a store that sells lawn mowers. Again, think of your audience and make an emotional appeal.

[ ]

Finally, make up a slogan for your city. The slogan should make residents feel proud of their city and should make other people want to visit your city.

[ ]

Images can make emotional appeals, as well, and most advertisements use a combination of words and images to persuade you to buy a product. Look back at the slogans you created. Choose your favorite and create an image to accompany it. Your slogan and image should work together to make a very strong emotional appeal. Create your ad in this space.

[ ]

Lesson 5 Order of Importance

When you write about events, you use time order. When you describe a place, you use spatial order. When you write to persuade, you should use order of importance.

Remember, when writers write to persuade, they try to make their readers think or act in a certain way. For example, you might try to persuade your principal to offer a Spanish class. As you persuade, you should save your most important ideas—your strongest arguments—for last. Build your ideas from least important to most important.

Here is part of a letter that Alissa wrote to her principal. Notice the reasons she gives for offering a Spanish class at her school.

Spanish would be a valuable addition to our school's course offerings. The need to speak and understand Spanish increases as the Hispanic population in the United States increases. Improved communication will help English-speaking and Spanish-speaking communities get along. Many jobs and opportunities are available for people who speak both English and Spanish. Educators agree that the best time to learn a language is when you are young. Statistics also indicate that learning a language can teach skills that transfer to other classes, resulting in better grades and test scores.

Alissa gave several reasons for why there should be a Spanish class at her school. Write them in order below from least important to most important.

_____

_____

_____

_____

_____

_____

_____

_____

Lesson 5 Order of Importance

What class do you think your school should add to its course offerings? Decide on a new class, then write a letter to your teacher or principal. Try to persuade the person that your idea is a good one. Ask yourself this: What will make this person want to support my idea?

Before you begin drafting your letter, write your reasons here. Then number them in the order in which you will use them in your letter. Save the strongest argument, or the most important reason, for last.

Reason: _____

Reason: _____

Reason: _____

Reason: _____

Dear _____,

Lesson 6 Letter of Complaint

A business letter is a letter written to a company, organization, or person you do not know. In a letter of complaint, the writer usually expresses a complaint, then asks the recipient to do something. It is important to be very clear about the action the recipient should take. Read this letter of complaint. Notice its six parts.

The **heading** includes the sender's address and the date.	814 Third Avenue Oak Park, IL 60302 June 27, 2008
The **inside address** is the name and address of the recipient.	Customer Service Department Publisher Warehouse 64417 Industrial Parkway West Chicago, IL 60624
A colon follows the **greeting**.	Dear Customer Service Department:

The text of the letter is the **body**.

I recently ordered one classroom set of *Speak Spanish Today* from Publisher Warehouse's catalog. The catalog item number is FL02245. The order number is 00-31944-20. The contents of my order, however, differ from what was indicated in the catalog. Instead of the 25 student workbooks I expected, I received only 20. My order also contained a set of classroom posters, which I was not expecting. They seem useful, however, and I would like to keep them.

Please send 5 additional *Speak Spanish Today* student workbooks, for which I have already paid, and please invoice me for the classroom posters. Their catalog item number is CP11281.

A comma follows the **closing**.

The sender always includes a **signature**.

Cordially,

Jenna Parkinson

Jenna Parkinson

Lesson 6 Letter of Complaint

Think of any kind of book and imagine that you ordered it from Publisher Warehouse. Then, imagine that the package arrives, but it contains the wrong book, the wrong number of books, or perhaps your order is damaged. Write a letter of complaint to Publisher Warehouse. Be sure to make a clear request at the end so the recipient knows what action you expect.

_____
_____
_____

Customer Service Department
Publisher Warehouse
64417 Industrial Parkway West
Chicago, IL 60624

Lesson 7 The Writing Process: Letter of Complaint

Use the writing process to plan and write a letter of complaint.

Prewrite

Think about things that you complain about. Maybe you even said, "I should write a letter to someone about this." Maybe the apples your mom bought at the grocery store turned rotten after just a day. Maybe the seam in your new shirt ripped out after just one washing. Make notes here about some things that you'd like to complain about.

_____   _____

_____   _____

_____   _____

Now, think about these issues for a few minutes. About which one do you feel strongly? Do you think that writing a letter of complaint would do any good? Choose the issue you will write about.

_____

Use this idea web to collect your reasons for complaining. Think about what happened and why you are unsatisfied. You may state opinions, but you must also give reasons or facts. Also, consider what action you expect the recipient to take. Add more ovals to the idea web if you need to.

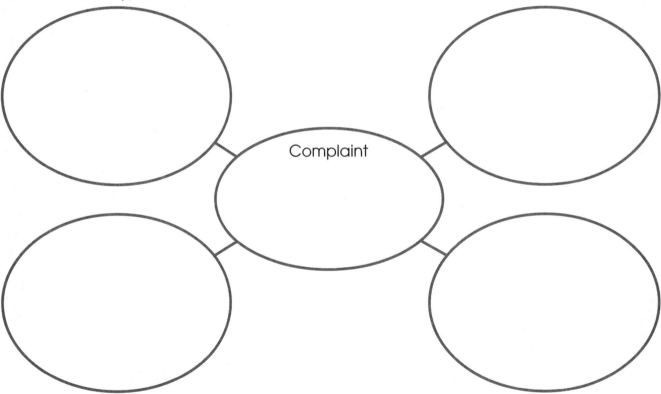

Lesson 7 The Writing Process: Letter of Complaint

Now, it is time to organize the points you will make in your letter of complaint. What is your strongest argument? Save that one for last. Write your important reasons or points in the boxes below. Then, number them in order.

Lesson 7 The Writing Process: Letter of Complaint

Draft

Write a first draft of your letter on this page. Refer to your chart on page 79. You may make up the recipient's address or get an actual address. As you write, don't worry about spelling or punctuation. Just get your ideas down in sentences and in order.

_____

_____

_____

_____

_____

_____

_____

_____

_____

_____

_____

_____

_____

_____

_____

_____

_____

_____

_____

_____

_____

_____

_____

_____

_____

Lesson 7 The Writing Process: Letter of Complaint

Revise

Even the most experienced writers read over their work and make changes. If possible, set your writing aside for a few hours. Then, reread your work slowly and carefully. Answer the questions below about your draft. If you answer "no" to any of these questions, those areas might need improvement. Feel free to make marks on your draft, so you know what needs more work.

- Did you state your complaint clearly?

- Did you give strong reasons to support your complaint?

- Did you organize those reasons in a logical order, such as least important to most important?

- What arguments might your audience make? Did you provide information to answer those arguments?

- Did you clearly state what action you want the letter's recipient to take?

- Did you use the correct business letter format?

Think carefully about your audience. With persuasive writing, it is especially important to aim your arguments right at your specific audience. Ask yourself these questions.

- What opinions does my audience already hold about this issue?

- What does my audience already know about this issue?

- What will they need to know in order to understand the issue?

- What emotional appeals might sway the audience in my direction?

It is always a good idea to read your work out loud at the revising stage. You might hear awkward sentences or ideas that don't flow quite right.

Lesson 7 The Writing Process: Letter of Complaint

Write your revised letter here. As you revise, remember to keep your audience in mind.

_____

_____

_____

_____

_____

_____

_____

_____

_____

_____

_____

_____

_____

_____

_____

_____

_____

_____

_____

_____

_____

_____

_____

_____

_____

_____

_____

_____

_____

_____

Lesson 7 The Writing Process: Letter of Complaint

Proofread

Now is the time to correct those last little mistakes. You will be a better proofreader if you look for just one kind of error at a time. Read first for capital letters, then read for end punctuation, then for spelling, and so on. Here is a checklist to use as you proofread your revised letter.

> _____ Each sentence begins with a capital letter.
>
> _____ Each sentence ends with the correct punctuation (period, question mark, or exclamation point).
>
> _____ Each sentence states a complete thought.
>
> _____ All words are spelled correctly. (If you're not sure, check a dictionary.)
>
> _____ Business letter format is correct.

When proofreaders work, they use certain symbols. These symbols will make your job easier.

Use these symbols as you proofread your letter. Remember to read your writing out loud, just like you did at the revising stage. You may hear mistakes or rough spots that you did not catch with your eyes.

- $\underset{\equiv}{\overset{C}{C}}$apitalize this letter.
- Write in a missing end mark like this: $_\odot$? !
- Add a comma$_\wedge$ please.
- Fix incorrect or misspelled words like ~~these~~ this.
- ~~Delete~~ this word.
- Lowercase this letter.

Publish

Write or type a final copy of your article on a separate sheet of paper. Work carefully and neatly so that there are no mistakes. If you feel strongly about the issue, ask permission to mail the letter.

Chapter 6
Lesson 1 Explanatory Writing

You read explanatory writing every day. Explanatory writing usually comes in the form of instructions. Some explanations are simple. A sign says "Use Other Door" and you know what to do. Some explanations are not simple. A new board game might come with a whole book full of instructions. A piece of furniture might come in a small box with instructions that help you assemble the parts.

Some explanations are not instructions, though. Some explanations tell how or why something happened. For example, your teacher might explain what events cause an earthquake. You might read an explanation of why people migrate from one continent to another.

List some explanations that you have read or heard this week.

_____   _____

_____   _____

Think about instructions you have read or used. How many different kinds can you list?

_____   _____   _____

_____   _____   _____

When you write to explain, or give instructions, you might write for these reasons:

- to tell how to make something
- to tell how something works
- to tell how to get somewhere
- to tell why something happened

Lesson 1 Explanatory Writing

Here is a simple explanation that tells how to make Judy's idea of the perfect piece of toast.

First, I toast a piece of whole wheat bread. I set the toaster on setting #1 because I like my bread lightly toasted. As soon as the toast pops up, I spread butter on it. This is important because the butter needs to melt. Then, I sprinkle cinnamon and sugar from the shaker onto the toast, right to the edges. It soaks into the melted butter and makes a delicious part of my breakfast.

The writer stated each step in order. To help readers follow the steps, she used order words such as *first*, *as soon as*, and *then* to make the order very clear. Underline each of those order words that you find in the paragraph.

What do you know how to do? Write down a few simple processes, such as making toast, that you can explain clearly.

_____   _____

_____   _____

Now, choose one of the processes you listed and think carefully about each of its steps. Imagine that you are explaining the process to someone who has never done it before. You'll have to start at the very beginning. List the steps here.

Process: _____

Step 1: _____

Step 2: _____

Step 3: _____

Step 4: _____

Step 5: _____

Step 6: _____

Step 7: _____

Step 8: _____

Step 9: _____

Step 10: _____

Step 11: _____

Step 12: _____

Lesson 2 Cause and Effect Relationships

Why are school buses yellow? Why is cheese orange? When you ask why, you are looking for causes. A **cause** is a reason why something happens. An **effect** is a thing that happens. Here are some examples of causes and effects. Think about the relationship between each cause and effect.

Cause	Effect
It is raining.	Track practice is held indoors.
The lawn mower is broken.	The grass is knee high.
Tamara broke a tooth.	She went to the dentist today.

When writers write to explain, they often use causes and effects. They use the words and phrases *so, because, as a result*, and *therefore* to link causes and effects. Read this paragraph about why earthquakes occur. Circle the cause-and-effect words and phrases in the paragraph below.

The surface of Earth consists of huge geologic plates. On these plates rest the oceans and continents. The place where two plates meet is called a *fault*. Sometimes, one plate or the other shifts, so they rub against each other at the fault line. If there is enough shifting, something has to give. Both plates may buckle, or one plate may slip up over the edge of the other. Whatever the type of movement, if it is significant, the surface of Earth shakes or heaves as a result.

Can you find some causes and effects in that paragraph? One is written for you. Write two other causes and effects.

Cause	Effect
Earth's plates shift.	The plates rub against each other.

Lesson 2 Cause and Effect Relationships

Writers might also use causes and effects when they tell about events that happened in a story or novel. Here are some causes and effects from *Hatchet* by Gary Paulsen.

> The pilot suffers a heart attack during the flight. As a result, Brian must land the plane. Though he does so successfully, he is hurt and alone in the wilderness. Brian must protect himself, so he builds a shelter and makes spears. He must eat, so he learns to spear fish. Because Brian uses his wits, he manages to survive.

Find the causes and effects in the paragraph above. Write them here. The first one is done for you.

Cause	Effect
The pilot suffers a heart attack.	Brian must land the plane.

Think about a story or novel you have read recently. What happened, and what did the characters do? Think about the events in terms of causes and effects. Ask yourself questions such as these: What caused this event to happen? What effect did this event have?

Write the causes and effects of some important events from the book.

Title: _____

Cause	Effect

Lesson 3 Report an Event

In a news report, a reporter writes about an event. The event might be a political convention, a traffic accident, or a warehouse explosion. In addition to relating events in the order in which they occurred, the reporter links causes and effects. Causes and effects help readers understand what happens and why.

Here is part of a report about a traffic accident. Look for words that signal cause-and-effect relationships: *so, because, as a result, therefore*. When you find them, circle them.

Car Crash on I-23

The vehicle, driven by Lincoln Marsh, age 37, went out of control because of an oil slick on the road surface. As a result, Marsh's vehicle left the roadway. Because the guardrail is being replaced, the temporary railing that was in place failed to stop the vehicle. The vehicle went down an embankment and lodged in the branches of a large tree. Mr. Marsh suffered only minor injuries. Since the temporary railing did not work, an investigation will be performed.

Write two causes and two effects from the paragraph.

Cause: _____   Effect: _____

_____   _____

_____   _____

Cause: _____   Effect: _____

_____   _____

_____   _____

Lesson 3 Report an Event

Now, think about causes and effects in an event in your own life. What happened yesterday? Even if nothing exciting happened, there were causes and effects in action. What did you do? What happened next? What resulted from these happenings? List some events in order. Draw arrows to show any cause-and-effect relationship among events.

1. _____

2. _____

3. _____

4. _____

5. _____

Now, practice writing about causes and effects. Write a paragraph about the happenings you listed above. Remember to use *so, because, as a result, therefore,* and other signal words to connect the cause-and-effect relationships.

_____

_____

_____

_____

_____

_____

_____

_____

_____

_____

_____

_____

_____

_____

_____

_____

Lesson 4 Graphics and Visual Aids

What is a picture worth? If you're putting together a bike, a picture to go along with the instructions can make the difference between success and failure. Sometimes, words can only do so much. Then, you need a picture to help out. Pictures can be drawings, photographs, maps, graphs, or diagrams.

The visual aid below shows a great deal of information, which saves the writer a lot of work.

A recent news article criticized the amount of money that Jennings County Schools spends on fuel and transportation. It is a fact that we spend 15% more on fuel and transportation than neighboring school districts. The reason is because our school district covers a wider area than most other school districts.

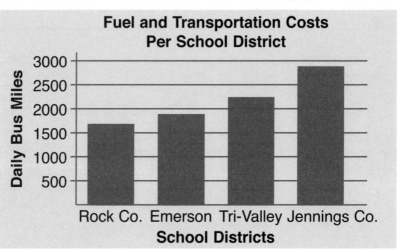

Graph the data below to help the Jennings County school superintendent prove that Jennings County has more students than nearby schools and, therefore, needs more money for school lunches. Use a bar graph similar to the one above.

School District	Enrollment
Jennings Co.	25,494 students
Emerson	17,239 students
Tri-Valley	16,117 students
Rock Co.	22,876 students

Lesson 4 Graphics and Visual Aids

A bar graph is just one way to show information in a visual way. Diagrams, circle graphs, and pictographs are also good tools. Here is a visual aid that shows how much money has been raised to build a new building for the humane society.

Now, create your own visual aid. Imagine that your class collected more canned food than several other classes for the school food drive. Think about how you could show that information in a creative and meaningful way. Make up data and write it in this space.

Now, create your visual aid here.

Lesson 5 Directions

A new student teacher stops you in the hall and asks for directions to the cafeteria. Can you give clear directions to help him find the way?

Directions need to be in order. As you write them, think about what happens first, second, next, and so on. In addition, directions need to tell where. Here are some words that are often used in directions.

Direction Words	Position Words	Order Words
left	over	first
right	under	second
up	past	then
down	beyond	next
north	before	after that
west	above	finally
	beside	

Mikayla told the new student teacher how to get to the cafeteria. Underline the direction, position, and order words in the paragraph.

> First, go down the big stairway at the end of the hall. At the bottom of the stairs, go straight. Go past the main entrance. Then, turn right and go down the blue hallway. At the end of that hall, look left, and you'll see the cafeteria beyond the big glass doors.

Lesson 5 Directions

Write directions that tell how to get from your classroom to the cafeteria. If you need to, close your eyes and imagine walking from here to there. Now, write your directions. If you need to, look back to page 92 for direction, position, and order words to use.

_____

_____

_____

_____

_____

_____

_____

_____

You have decided to invite friends to visit you in your remote mountain cabin. They will have to hike up the mountain from the nearest village. Write directions so they can find the way. If you wish, make a sketch of this make-believe path. Then, write the directions here.

_____

_____

_____

_____

_____

_____

_____

_____

_____

_____

Lesson 6 The Writing Process: How-to Instructions

You may be called upon at any time to explain how to do something. Maybe a friend wants to know how to finish level 19 of your favorite computer game. Perhaps someone asks you to explain the rules of wrestling. Use the writing process to see how good you are at explaining to someone else how to do something.

Prewrite

Think about things that you know how to do. You might know how to make a great after-school snack, or maybe you can shape balloons into amazing animals. Write down some things that you know how to do.

_____   _____

_____   _____

_____   _____

Look over your list and imagine explaining how to do each thing. With which topic are you most comfortable? Explore the idea by writing down everything you can think of about that topic.

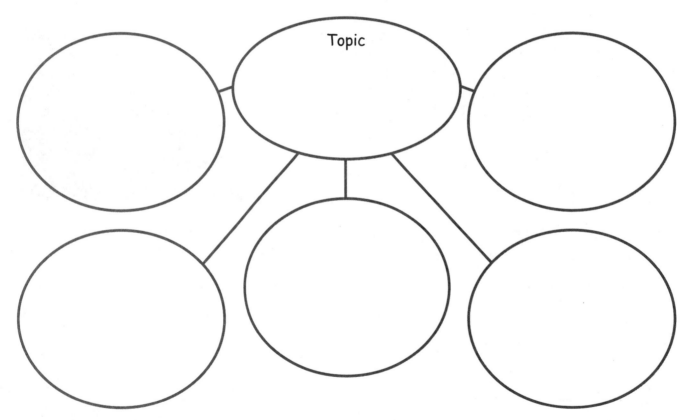

Are you comfortable with your topic? If not, go back to your list and choose another. Explore it with an idea web on a separate sheet of paper. Remember to think about your audience. What will they need to know?

Lesson 6 The Writing Process: How-to Instructions

Now, it is time to put the steps in order. Think about the process you are about to explain. Assume that your audience has never done this before, so you need to start at the very beginning. Use the sequence chart on this page to list the important steps in your explanation. Don't worry about details here; just be sure to list the main steps in the correct order.

1. _____

2. _____

3. _____

4. _____

5. _____

6. _____

7. _____

8 _____

9. _____

Lesson 6 The Writing Process: How-to Instructions

Draft

In the space below, write a first draft of your instructions. Keep your sequence chart on hand as you write. Continue on another sheet of paper if you need to. As you write, don't worry about getting everything perfect. Just get your ideas down in sentences and in order.

_____

_____

_____

_____

_____

_____

_____

_____

_____

_____

_____

_____

_____

_____

_____

_____

_____

_____

_____

_____

_____

_____

Lesson 6 The Writing Process: How-to Instructions

Revise

For many writers, revising is much more difficult than writing the first draft. Reread your work with fresh eyes. Answer the questions below about your draft. If you answer "no" to any of these questions, those areas might need improvement. Make marks on your draft so you know what needs more work.

- Did you explain how to do something from beginning to end?

- Did you include all of the steps in order?

- Did you include time-order words to make the sequence clear?

- Did you use direction and position words to make your details clear?

- Did you use good describing words so your readers can "see" what they are supposed to do?

- Did you keep your audience in mind by asking yourself what they might already know or what they need to know?

- Did you include a heading or title so readers know what they are reading about?

Recognizing causes and effects helps readers understand what they are reading. The words *so, because, therefore,* and *as a result* may signal a cause-effect relationship. Here is an example:

Slam the clay against the tabletop. This removes air bubbles from the clay. Continue working the clay so that it becomes soft. Do not fold the clay or poke your fingers into it because that would result in new air bubbles.

Look back at your draft and think about cause-and-effect relationships. Are the causes and effects clear? Do you need to add signal words to make them more clear?

Lesson 6 The Writing Process: How-to Instructions

Write the revision of your first draft here. As you revise, remember to think about important details that your readers will need to know.

_____
_____
_____
_____
_____
_____
_____
_____
_____
_____
_____
_____
_____
_____
_____
_____
_____
_____
_____
_____
_____
_____
_____
_____
_____
_____

Lesson 6 The Writing Process: How-to Instructions

Proofread

Now is the time to correct any last little mistakes. You will be a better proofreader if you look for just one kind of error at a time. Read through once for capital letters. Read again for end punctuation, spelling, and so on. Here is a checklist to use as you proofread your instructions.

____ Each sentence begins with a capital letter.

____ Each sentence ends with the correct punctuation (period, question mark, or exclamation point).

____ Each sentence states a complete thought.

____ All words are spelled correctly. (If you're not sure, check a dictionary.)

Use standard proofreading symbols as you proofread your own revised instructions.

As you proofread, remember to read your writing out loud, even if there is no one to listen. When you read, you may hear mistakes or awkward spots that you did not see.

- Ꞔapitalize this letter.
- Add a missing end mark: ⊙ ? !
- Insert a comma please.
- Fix incorᵣect or misspelled words.
- Delete this word.
- Lowercase this ℒetter.

Publish

Write a final copy of your instructions on a separate sheet of paper. Write or type carefully and neatly so that there are no mistakes. If you wish, include a graph, chart, or diagram to enhance your instructions and to make them more clear. Read your instructions out loud, or perform a demonstration in front of an audience.

Chapter 7
Lesson 1 Informational Writing

When your teachers assign a report, they are asking you to inform them about what you know or have learned. When you write to inform, you present information about a topic. Here is a report that Ashley wrote about linen.

Linen

Three centuries ago, clothing made of linen was fairly common. Hard-working colonists in North America wore it at work and play. Today, linen fabric is likely to be made into sporty or dressy clothing, but never work clothing.

Linen fabric was familiar to the early Americans because it was in use throughout Europe. Once they migrated to North America, it was costly to import fabric, so the colonists learned to make their own. To do so, they had to raise a crop of flax.

To make linen, a farmer first harvests the flax plants. He wants the fibers to be as long as possible, so he pulls the plants rather than cut them. The stems are then soaked in water for as long as three weeks. This loosens the inner fibers. Then, the flax is dried and passed through rollers to separate the useful inner fiber from the tough part of the stem. Next, the stems are beaten to free the fibers from the unwanted parts. Finally, the fibers are hackled, or combed, to clean and straighten the desirable fibers. After hackling, the fiber is ready to be spun into thread, then woven into fabric.

The type of linen fabric that results depends on the quality of the fibers and the care taken during processing. If the fiber is coarse, it may be made into rope, canvas, or carpet backing. If the fiber is fine, it may be woven into fabric for fine clothing, or it may become the most delicate of handkerchiefs. The role of linen has changed, but it is still an important fabric that contributes to our daily lives.

Lesson 1 Informational Writing

When writers write to inform, they use transition words to connect ideas. **Transition words** help readers understand connections among ideas. Here are some common transition words:

again	before long	in addition
also	but	in spite of
and	consequently	therefore
as a result	finally	thus
at the same time	for example	when
because	however	

Look back at Ashley's report on page 100. Find the transition words that she used. Circle them.

Now, explore what you could write a report about. It is always a good idea to choose a topic in which you are interested. If you are studying world history and you think pyramids are boring, don't choose pyramids for your topic. Instead, choose to write about Greek myths or the products that were traded on the Silk Road. To help you think of possible topics, answer these questions.

What are some places in the world that interest you or that you would like to visit?

_____   _____   _____

_____   _____   _____

What are some historical places or events that you know about? It might be an ancient city, a battleground, or a historical person's home.

_____   _____

_____   _____

Here are the features of informational writing:

- It gives important information about a topic.

- It presents a main idea, which is supported with facts.

- It may include information from several different sources.

- It draws a conclusion based on the information presented.

- It is organized in a logical way. Transition words connect ideas.

Lesson 2 Facts, Opinions, and Bias

You already know what facts and opinions are. Facts can be proven to be true. Opinions are judgments that people make. What about bias?

Bias is an unfair "slant" that a writer gives to a topic. Some writers may do it by accident. Perhaps they have such strong views that they don't realize they are presenting only one point of view or only a portion of the facts. Other writers bias their work on purpose to present their own views and to persuade others to believe as they do.

Can you find the bias—the unfair slant—in this portion of a review article about sewing machines?

> This year's new sewing machine models all offer similar features. The SewGood 207T, with a colorful array of buttons, is dizzying in its options. The heavy Marvel XD looks plain by comparison, though it has the same mind-numbing selection of features. One has to look for them on an LCD screen. The EverSeam 1601 looks just like your mother's machine, but has all the features you want for today's fabrics and projects.

The first sentence tells us that both machines have "similar features." However, the first is "dizzying," and the second is "heavy," "plain," and "mind-numbing." The third, however, is "just like your mother's machine." A reader certainly comes away thinking that the third machine is the best of the bunch.

How could this writer have avoided bias? Consider some replacements for the words that send negative messages. For example, she could have used *dazzling* instead of *dizzying*. For the second model, she could have omitted *heavy* and used *vast array* instead of *mind-numbing selection*. Can you think of other changes that would remove bias from the review? Write them here.

Original Word or Phrase

_____

_____

_____

_____

Replacement Word or Phrase

_____

_____

_____

_____

Lesson 2 Facts, Opinions, and Bias

It is important for readers to recognize bias when they see it. Advertisements often include bias, which is one method of persuasion. News stories might contain bias, which could lead readers to misunderstand an issue. It is important to think about what is fact and what is opinion, and to ask whether all sides of an issue are being fairly presented. As a writer, you should ask the same questions.

Suppose that you are to review some products. You might compare two cell phones, two versions of a video game, or two recordings by your favorite group. Write a fair, unbiased review of the products. Tell what is both good and bad about each product. Remember, in a review, your job is not only to say what you like but to evaluate the products. In the evaluation, you should state both facts, such as "The new model has more features than the old model," and opinions, such as "I find the old model's screen easier to read."

_____

_____

_____

_____

_____

_____

_____

_____

_____

_____

_____

_____

_____

_____

_____

_____

_____

_____

_____

_____

Lesson 3 Reliable Sources

Information is everywhere around you. You can get information from a book, from a Web site, and even from a cell phone. Which sources of information are best? How can you tell which are good and which are not good?

First, think about the kinds of sources available. For each question, write the source that would be most useful based on the type of information required. For some questions, more than one source might be useful.

dictionary newspaper atlas	print encyclopedia online encyclopedia	almanac Web site

_____ What is the world record for the high jump?

_____ How many acres of rain forest exist today?

_____ When did the Crusades occur?

_____ Where is the Yangtze River?

_____ What did the school board discuss at its monthly meeting?

_____ What does *jargon* mean?

_____ What kinds of ancient historical artifacts have been found on the island of Crete?

Lesson 3 Reliable Sources

Once you find a source that seems to have the information you need, you must decide whether the source is reliable. If the source is printed, ask yourself these questions:

- **When was this source published?** If you need current information, the source should be only one or two years old. Depending on the subject, even that might be too old.

- **Who wrote this source and for what purpose?** If the source is an encyclopedia, atlas, or almanac, you can be pretty confident that responsible authors wrote it to provide information. If it is a magazine article or a work of nonfiction, you need to ask more questions. Might there be bias in the material? Read the book jacket or an "About the Author" blurb to discover as much as you can about the expertise of the author and the purpose for writing.

If you are looking at an online source, there are some other questions to ask. Keep in mind that anyone can create a Web site. Just because you see information on a Web site does not mean that it is accurate.

- **What person or organization established or maintains this Web site? What is the purpose of the site?** What makes this person or organization an expert on the topic?

- **What is the purpose of the site?** Whether a person or an organization maintains a site, there is the potential for bias. Does the person or organization want to inform, to sell something, or to present a certain point of view (which may or may not be biased)?

- **When was the site last updated?** Just as with print sources, the publication date may matter, depending on whether you need current information.

Write *yes* or *no* to indicate whether these sources would be reliable.

_____ You are writing about a recent natural disaster. You consult a report on the National Weather Service's Web site.

_____ You are writing about Egypt's pyramids and how they were built. You refer to an article in a history magazine that was published 18 years ago.

_____ You are writing an article about testing in schools. You go to your state's Department of Education Web site to collect data.

_____ You are writing an article on skateboard safety. You cite www.Kensboards.com, which is a site that sells custom-make skateboards.

Lesson 4 Taking Notes

Taking notes is what you do when you collect information for a report or presentation. Once you locate the information, your job is first to skim to make sure the source is what you need. Then, you must read carefully. Finally, you must paraphrase, or briefly state in your own words, what you have read and record it on note cards or in a writing notebook.

Eric is writing a report on Maine. Here is one of his note cards.

The People

population: about 1.4 million (2000 census)
capital: Augusta
largest cities (in order): Portland, Lewiston, Bangor, Auburn, South Portland, Augusta, Brunswick

Maine: A State's Story, pages 14, 17

Eric's note card has three important parts. First, at the top he listed the topic. He knows that one part of his report will be about the people in the state. He marks each note card with a specific topic. Labeling the cards in that way will make organizing them and writing his draft much easier.

Second, Eric wrote his notes. They are very brief. He included only the most important pieces of information.

Finally, he wrote the name of the source and the page numbers where the information came from. If he needs to go back and check a fact or get more information, he can do it easily.

Lesson 4 Taking Notes

Your assignment is to write a report about a state. You are to include sections on the land, the people, history, and business and industry. Find an article about a state of your choice in a print or an online source. Then, take some notes. Label each card with one of the sections listed above. Remember to keep your notes brief and to list your source at the bottom of each card.

Lesson 5 Using an Outline

An **outline** is a way to organize information. If you are writing a report, it is an excellent step to take during your prewriting stage. After you collect information and take notes, you can outline the information to make sure you have everything you need.

Eric has begun his outline about Maine.

Maine

I. The Land
    A. Location
        1. bordered on north by Quebec and New Brunswick, Canada
        2. bordered on west by New Hampshire
        3. bordered along southeast by Atlantic Ocean
    B. Regions
        1. White Mountains
        2. New England Upland
        3. Seaboard Lowland
    C. Climate
        1. short summers; long, cold winters
        2. growing season 100–180 days
        3. 36–46 inches rainfall per year
II. The People
    A. Early People
        1. Abnaki
        2. French Canadians

Eric started out with his first main idea: The Land. Indented under that main idea are three topics: Location, Region, and Climate. Within each topic, Eric listed supporting details. Note that this format is called a **topic outline**. The information is recorded in short words and phrases.

Lesson 5 Using an Outline

Look back at the note cards you created on page 107. Create part of an outline from those notes. Go back to the source if you need additional information. Remember, the format and the labels look like this:

I. Main Idea

    A. Topic

        1. Supporting detail

        2. Supporting detail

Lesson 6 Citing Sources

The last page of a report includes a **bibliography**, or a list of the sources used. The bibliography shows readers what sources you used and allows them to consult those sources if they want further information. It also shows your teacher that you used a variety of sources and made good choices.

In a bibliography, you need to give certain specific information so that another person could locate that same source. Each type of source has a slightly different format. Here are examples of bibliographic entries for the most common types of sources. If, for any entry, you don't have a piece of information, just skip it and go on to the next piece of information. Pay close attention to punctuation. Periods, commas, quotation marks, and underlining are all part of the format.

Encyclopedia (print or CD-ROM)

Author (if given) last name, first name. "Title of Article." Title of Encyclopedia. Year published. Volume number, page number.

> "Maine." Encyclopaedia Britannica. 1992. Volume 13, 804–805.

Book

Author last name, first name. Title of Book. Place of Publication: Publisher, date of publication.

> Pendleton, Tom. Maine: A State's Story. Portland: Maine State Historical Society, 2004.

Magazine article

Author last name, first name. "Title of Article." Title of Magazine. data of magazine: page numbers of article.

> Swift, Marcy. "Portland's Heritage." Travel Maine. June 14, 2005, 34–38.

Web site

Author last name, first name (if given). "Title of Article or Page." Sponsor of Web site. Date of article. Web site address (URL)

> Altman, Angela. "Maine in June." Portland Visitors' Organization. April 2005. www.portlandmaine.org

NOTE: There is no period at the end of the Web site citation.

Lesson 6 Citing Sources

Now, create bibliographic entries of your own. Locate one source of each type. They don't all have to be about the same topic. What's important is that you practice using the format for each type of source.

Encyclopedia

_____

_____

_____

Book

_____

_____

_____

Magazine article

_____

_____

_____

Web site

_____

_____

_____

Lesson 7 Writing about Problems and Solutions

One way to organize a report is to use a problem-solution approach. Not all topics fit this type of format, but many do. While Eric studied Maine for his social studies class, he learned about whippoorwills, a woodland bird that is native to Maine. For science class, he wrote a report on whippoorwills. Here is the problem-solution chart he made as part of his prewriting stage.

Problem:
Whippoorwill populations are decreasing due to loss of their woodland habitat.

Possible solutions:
1. Stop destroying woodland habitat
   control development
2. Set aside some woodland habitat
   woodland preservation
   woodland management

Recommended solution:
Educate people about the importance of preserving woodland habitat. It is the only habitat in which these birds can survive.

When Eric writes his report, he will state the problem, then explore each possible solution. Finally, he will state his recommended solution and give reasons why it is the best solution to the problem.

Lesson 7 Writing about Problems and Solutions

Think of a topic that interests you. It might be about an animal species that is disappearing, like the whippoorwill. Or it could be a local issue, such as pollution or the possible destruction of a historic building. Complete the problem-solution chart on this page.

Problem:

Possible solutions:

Recommended solution:

Lesson 8 The Writing Process: Informational Writing

Writing a report is a good way to show what you know. It is also a good way to learn about a topic that interests you. Use the writing process to plan and write a report.

Prewrite

Look back at the topic ideas you recorded on page 101. Which one seems most interesting? Choose one and begin to explore that topic with the help of this chart.

Topic: _____

What I Know	What I Want to Know	How or Where I Might Find Out Information

If you are comfortable with this subject, conduct some research and take notes. Remember to organize your note cards by specific topic. For example, Eric organized his whippoorwill note cards in these categories: problem, possible solution 1, possible solution 2, possible solution 3, recommended solution.

Lesson 8 The Writing Process: Informational Writing

Now, it is time to focus on putting ideas in order. Think about your topic. How should information be organized? By cause and effect? In order of importance? In problem-solution format? Looking at and organizing your note cards might help you decide. List your main points or ideas in order on this page.

Subject: _____

Lesson 8 The Writing Process: Informational Writing

Draft

It is time to write a first draft of your report. Keep your notes and the chart on page 115 nearby as you write. Write your draft on this page. Continue on another sheet of paper if you need to. As you write, don't worry about misspelling words or getting everything perfect. Just get your ideas down in sentences and paragraphs.

_____

_____

_____

_____

_____

_____

_____

_____

_____

_____

_____

_____

_____

_____

_____

_____

_____

_____

_____

_____

_____

_____

_____

_____

Lesson 8 The Writing Process: Informational Writing

Revise

Every writer can improve his or her work. Pick up your report and read it as if you are seeing it for the first time. Remember, even experienced writers feel that revising is much more difficult than writing the first draft.

Answer the questions below about your draft. If you answer "no" to any of these questions, those areas might need improvement. Feel free to make marks on your draft, so you know what needs more work.

- Did you present information clearly and in a logical order?
- Does each paragraph consist of a main idea supported by facts?
- Did you include transition words to connect ideas?
- Did you begin with a sentence that will make readers want to keep going?
- Did you use information from several different sources?
- Did you draw a conclusion based on the information presented?
- Did you use your own words to state facts?
- Did you keep your audience in mind by asking yourself what they might already know or what they need to know?
- Did you present a fair and balanced view of the subject?

Here are a few pointers about making your report interesting to read.

- Vary the length of your sentences. Mixing short, medium, and long sentences keeps your readers interested.
- Vary the style of your sentences. Begin sentences with different kinds of words or clauses. For example, begin some sentences with verbs, some with phrases (such as "In a woodland habitat,"), and some with clauses (such as "Because the whippoorwill population is decreasing,").

On page 118, write the revision of your draft. As you revise, pay special attention to the length and style of your sentences.

Lesson 8 The Writing Process: Informational Writing

_____

_____

_____

_____

_____

_____

_____

_____

_____

_____

_____

_____

_____

_____

_____

_____

_____

_____

_____

_____

_____

_____

_____

_____

_____

_____

_____

Lesson 8 The Writing Process: Informational Writing

Proofread

Now is the time to correct those last little mistakes. Proofreading is easier if you look for just one kind of error at a time. Read through once for capital letters. Read again for end punctuation, spelling, and so on. Use this checklist as you proofread your report.

> ____ Each sentence begins with a capital letter.
>
> ____ Each sentence states a complete thought and ends with the correct punctuation (period, question mark, or exclamation point).
>
> ____ All proper nouns begin with capital letters.
>
> ____ All words are spelled correctly.

Use standard proofreading symbols as you proofread your revised report.

Remember to read your writing out loud during the proofreading stage. You may hear a mistake or an awkward spots that you did not see.

> - Capitalize this letter.
> - Add a missing end mark: ? !
> - Add a comma please.
> - Fix incorect or misspelled words.
> - Delete this word.
> - Lowercase this Letter.

Publish

Write or type a final copy of your report on a separate sheet of paper. Write carefully and neatly so that there are no mistakes. Make a cover page for the front and a bibliography for the end. Read your report out loud to the class.

Writer's Handbook

Parts of Speech

A **noun** is a word that names a person, place, or thing. Common nouns name general things. Proper nouns name specific things and always begin with a capital letter.

Common Nouns	Proper Nouns
officer	Sergeant Rhimes
racehorse	Seattle Slew
park	Yellowstone National Park
store	Becker Hardware

A **verb** is an action word. Verbs also show a state of being. Every complete sentence has at least one verb. Verbs show action in the past, in the present, and in the future.

Last week, my team *lost*.
I *was* sad about the loss.
Today, my team *plays* against Sutherland.
Next week, we *will play* at Hinton.

An **adjective** modifies, or describes, a noun or pronoun. Adjectives tell *what kind, how much* or *how many*, or *which one*.

The *brick* building is the Community Center. *(what kind)*
It has *two* entrances. *(how many)*
I usually use *this* entrance. *(which one)*

An **adverb** modifies a verb, an adjective, or another adverb. Adverbs tell *how, when, where*, or *to what degree*.

We planned the parade *carefully*. *(how)*
We chose the date *already*. *(when)*
The parade route will go *there*. *(where)*
We are *completely* prepared. *(to what degree)*

Writer's Handbook

Punctuation

End marks on sentences show whether a sentence is a statement, a command, a question, or an exclamation.

> This sentence makes a statement.
> Make your bed, please.
> Why might you want to ask a question?
> I can't believe how excited you are!

Commas help keep ideas clear.

> In a list or series: The parade had floats, bands, and old cars.
> In a compound sentence: I waved at my dad, but I'm not sure he saw me.
> After an introductory phrase or clause: After the parade, we all had ice cream.
> To separate a speech tag: I said to Dad, "Did you see me?"

Quotation marks show the exact words that a speaker says. They enclose the speaker's words and the punctuation that goes with the words.

> "Sure, I saw you," Dad said. "How could I have missed that red hat?"
> "That's exactly why I wore it," I said.

Colons are used to introduce a series, to set off a clause, for emphasis, in time, and in business letter greetings.

> My favorite vegetables include the following: *broccoli, red peppers, and spinach.* (series)

> The radio announcer said: *"The game is postponed due to rain."* (clause)

> The skiers expected the worst as they got off the mountain: *an avalanche.* (emphasis)

Writer's Handbook

The Writing Process

When writers write, they take certain steps. Those steps make up the writing process.

Step 1: Prewrite

First, writers choose a topic. Then, they collect and organize ideas or information. They might write their ideas in a list. They might also make a chart and begin to put their ideas in some kind of order.

Tomika is going to write about her dance lessons. She put her ideas in a web.

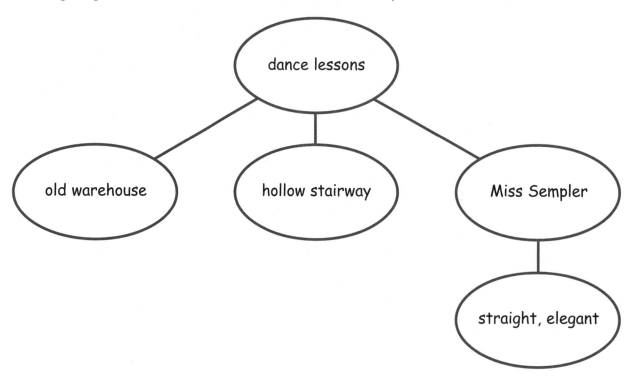

Step 2: Draft

Next, writers put their ideas on paper in a first draft. Writers know that there might be mistakes in this first draft. That's okay. Here is Tomika's first draft.

> Every Wednesday after school I eagerly climb the hollow stairway of the old Benson's Warehouse building I am glad to go dance lessons, even if they are in an old warehouse. Miss Sempler always greets the other students and me. She is so straight and elagant. She says we sound like a heard of hippoes coming up the stairs. I try to go up the stairs with my head high and my shoulders back, just like miss Sempler would.

Writer's Handbook

Step 3: Revise

Then, writers change or fix their first draft. They might decide to move ideas around or to add information. They might also take out words or sentences that don't belong. Here are Tomika's changes.

> Every Wednesday after school I eagerly climb the hollow, echoing stairway of the old Benson's Warehouse building I am glad to go to dance lessons, even if they are in an old warehouse. Miss Sempler always greets the other students and me at the top of the stairs. She is so straight and elagant. She says we sound like a heard of hippoes coming up the stairs. I try to go up the stairs with my head high and my shoulders back, just like miss Sempler would. I almost feel like a dancer even before I get to class.

Step 4: Proofread

Writers usually write a new copy so their writing is neat. Then, they read again to make sure everything is correct. They read for mistakes in their sentences. Tomika found several more mistakes when she proofread her work.

> Every Wednesday after school, I eagerly climb the hollow, echoing stairway of the old Benson's Warehouse building. I am glad to go to dance lessons, even if they are in an old warehouse. Miss Sempler always greets the other students and me at the top of the stairs. She is so straight and elegant. She says we sound like a heard of hippoes coming up the stairs. I try to go up the stairs with my head high and my shoulders back, just like miss Sempler would. I almost feel like a dancer even before I get to class.

Step 5: Publish

Finally, writers make a final copy that has no mistakes. They are now ready to share their writing with a reader. They might choose to read their writing out loud. They can also add pictures and create a book. There are many ways for writers to publish, or to share, their work with readers.

Writer's Handbook

Personal Narrative

In a personal narrative, a writer writes about something he has done or seen. A personal narrative can be about anything, as long as the writer is telling about one of his or her own experiences. Here is the final version of Tomika's paragraph about dance lessons.

Words that tell time indicate when something happens.	Every Wednesday after school I eagerly climb the hollow, echoing stairway of the old Benson's Warehouse building. I am glad to go to dance lessons, even if they are in an old warehouse. Miss Sempler always greets the other students and me at the top of the stairs. She is so straight and elegant. She says we sound like a herd of hippos coming up the stairs. I try to go up the stairs with my head high and my shoulders back, just like Miss Sempler would. I almost feel like a dancer even before I get to class.	The words *I* and *me* show that the writer is part of the action.
Describing words and figurative language help readers "see" or "hear" what is happening.		The writer stayed on topic. All of the sentences give information about Tomika's dance lesson.

Descriptive Writing

When writers describe, they might tell about an object, a place, or an event. They use sensory words so that readers can see, hear, smell, feel, or taste whatever is being described. In this example of descriptive writing, Brad described the results of his science experiment.

The writer uses the whole-to-whole comparison method. He describes one plant in this paragraph, and the other plant in the next paragraph.	Daisy plant A was my control plant. It received the same amount of water as plant B, but it received no Epsom salts. Plant A has 9 leaves and is 12.5 inches tall. Its leaves are bright green, and it has a healthy appearance. Daisy plant B received two doses of Epsom salts. The first dose was administered just as the first leaves appeared, and the second was administered one week later. Plant B has 14 leaves and is 14 inches tall. This plant also has 2 flower buds. The leaves are a deep green, and the plant is fuller and has a more pleasing appearance than does daisy plant A.	Sensory details help readers visualize the scene.
		The writer gives information in the same order in each paragraph.

Writer's Handbook

Fiction Stories

Writers write about made-up things. They might write about people or animals. The story might seem real, or it might seem unreal, or fantastic. Here is a story that Jason wrote. It has human characters, and the events could really happen, so Jason's story is realistic.

	Bitter Victory	
The story has a beginning, a middle, and an end.	Coach had put Neil out on the field. He hadn't played all season. Neil suspected that Coach felt sorry for him, but he was glad to be in the game. Not that he figured anything would actually happen. But then, there was the ball. A Hampton player had fumbled it, and fumbled it badly. It was skittering crazily across the chewed-up grass. Now, it was coming right at him.	The first paragraph establishes the setting.
This story is written in third-person point of view. The narrator is not a part of the action. So, words such as *he*, *she*, *her*, *him*, and *they* refer to the characters.	Neil picked up the ball and looked frantically all around him. There was a lot of confusion. Without his realizing it, Neil's feet were moving. No one was taking much notice. He crouched down a little to hide the ball tucked under his arm. He made his feet go faster and headed for the end zone. He gritted his teeth, expecting to get clobbered. Forty…thirty…twenty…ten…*Whumpf!* A Hampton player caught him at the last moment. The impact sent Neil careening forward. He stumbled over the line, completely out of control. A sting in his ankle was quickly forgotten; Neil tasted dirt and grass as he rolled and finally came to a stop. Grinning at his approaching teammates, Neil yelled, "We won! We won!" Neil's teammates were all yelling at him, but not about winning the game. Neil looked down at his ankle, which was bent at a nauseating angle. A blur of noises and movements occurred as Neil was loaded onto a stretcher and carried off. What he remembered, though, was the scoreboard, and the fact that the crowd went wild, just like in the movies.	Sensory words help readers visualize what is happening. Time and order words keep ideas clear.

Informational Writing

When writers write to inform, they present information about a topic. Informational writing is nonfiction. It is not made up; it contains facts.

Here is a paragraph from a report about the Olympics.

	The Olympics	
The writer states the main idea in a topic sentence. It is the first sentence of the paragraph.	The tradition of the Olympics is a long and honorable one. The first Olympics were played in Greece more than 2,500 years ago. The initial contest was held in 776 B.C. There was just one event—a footrace. Later, the Greeks added boxing, wrestling, chariot racing, and the pentathlon. The ancient Games were held every four years for more than a thousand years.	These sentences contain details that support the main idea. A time-order word connects ideas.

Writer's Handbook

Explanatory (or How-to) Writing

When writers explain how to do things, they might tell how to make a craft, play a computer game, or use a cell phone. Tony has written instructions for Jenna, who is going to take care of Tony's hamster while he is on vacation.

The first sentence summarizes the care instructions.

Order words help readers keep the steps in order.

> Each day when you come, there are three things to do. First check Heidi's water to make sure the bottle hasn't fallen out of place. Then fill her food dish. Her food is in the green bag next to the cage. Finally play with Heidi. She would love to snuggle in your neck and maybe crawl down your sleeve.

Clear words help readers understand the instructions.

Persuasive Writing

In persuasive writing, writers try to make readers think, feel, or act in a certain way. Persuasive writing shows up in newspaper and magazine articles, letters to the editor, business letters, and, of course, advertisements. Trina has written a letter to the editor of her school newsletter.

The writer begins by stating her opinion.

The writer uses an emotional appeal to persuade readers to agree with her.

Dear Editor:
  The locker bay is a mess. So many of the lockers are old, scratched, and dented. Some of them don't even close properly. How can we be proud of our school when the locker room is falling apart? More importantly, the worn-out lockers seem to encourage students to mistreat them even further. Someone needs to repair or replace the lockers so that we can feel good about our school.
Trina Hardesty

The writer states facts to lend support to her opinions.

The writer includes a specific request for action.

Writer's Handbook

Business Letters

Writers write business letters to people or organizations with whom they are not familiar. Business letters usually involve a complaint or a request for information. Mariko needs information for a school report. She wrote a business letter to request information.

> **The heading includes the sender's address and the date.**

8213 Rivera Boulevard
Fredericksburg, TX 78624
March 4, 2008

> **The inside address is the complete name and address of the recipient.**

Dr. Olivia Lamas, DVM
Lamas Animal Clinic
944 Curry Lane
Fredericksburg, TX 78624

Dear Dr. Lamas:

> **A colon follows the greeting.**

> **The text of the letter is the body.**

My class is exploring careers this month. I would like to learn about being a veterinarian. Is there a time when I can visit your office? I have many questions, and I would like to watch you work with the animals.

Please call my teacher, Ms. Zapata, to set up a time that is convenient for you. The school's phone number is 830-555-0021.

Thank you for your help, and I look forward to meeting you.

Sincerely,

> **A comma follows the closing.**

> **The sender always includes a signature.**

Mariko Campillo
Mariko Campillo

Answer Key

Chapter 1

Lesson 1

Page 5
Topic sentence: My grandmother is one
  of those people who has her holiday
  shopping done by September.
Details:
She picks out gifts when she and
  Grandpa travel. She goes to local stores
  when they have good sales during the
  summer.

Page 6
Possible main idea: Shopping can be
  annoying.
Paragraphs will vary.

Lesson 2

Page 7
There is a movie display outside on the
  grass next to a forest.
Main ideas will vary.

Page 8
Underlined topic sentence: For a city kid,
  country life can be a little alarming.
Crossed-out sentence: Possums are not
  even in the same family as rats.
Details will vary.
Paragraphs will vary.

Lesson 3

Page 10
Order of steps shown:
Step 4: Proofread
Step 5: Publish
Step 1: Prewrite
Step 3: Revise
Step 2: Draft

Lesson 4

Page 11
Possible purposes for writing:
news article—to inform, to explain
personal narrative—to inform, to explain
story—to entertain
business letter—to inform, to persuade

Lesson 5

Page 13
Suggestions may include describing
  warm-ups, explaining how teams should
  be picked, the rules or set-up for dodge
  ball, what freeze tag is, and what
  "centers" are.
Instructions to substitute teacher will vary.

Lesson 6

Page 14
Details will vary.
Paragraphs will vary.

Page 15
Revised, proofread, and rewritten
  paragraphs will vary.

Answer Key

Chapter 2

Lesson 1

Page 17
Responses to idea-starters will vary.

Lesson 2

Page 18
Time words and phrases will vary.
Sentences will vary.

Page 19
Circled words in paragraph: *A week later,*
As soon as, Then
Paragraphs will vary.

Lesson 3

Page 21
<u>Steve</u> viewed the exhibit.
X The <u>exhibit</u> was lit with special lights.
<u>Elijah</u> was looking at one display.
X <u>Visitors</u> were entertained by a pianist.
Sentences will vary.

Lesson 4

Page 22
Ideas and idea webs will vary.

Page 23
Entries in sequence charts will vary.

Page 24
Drafts will vary.

Page 26
Revisions will vary.

Answer Key

Chapter 3

Lesson 1

Page 28
Possible details:
See: white sleeve, head down, caramel
   hanging on my chin
Hear: Scruunnch
Smell: rich, sweet caramel
Touch: juices flowed, gooey brown
   caramel, sticky mess
Taste: juices flowed; rich, sweet caramel;
   tartness

Page 29
Details and paragraphs will vary.

Lesson 2

Page 30
Possible revised sentence: An impatient
   driver blew his noisy horn.

Page 31
Possible revised sentences:
A driver blew his horn angrily.
The trucks roll noisily to a stop at the
   corner.
The cab of a big truck can be amazingly
   comfortable.
Trucks move goods efficiently across the
   entire country.

Lesson 3

Page 32
Circled spatial words: *past, Through,*
   above, beyond, higher
Spatial descriptions will vary.

Page 33
Descriptive paragraphs will vary.

Lesson 4

Page 34
Details and paragraphs will vary.

Page 35
Details and paragraphs will vary.

Lesson 5

Page 36
One bed is lumpier than the other.
That bed must be more uncomfortable
   than the other.
I would rather sleep on the neater bed.
Sentences will vary.

Page 37
Comparative sentences will vary.
smarter, tallest, happiest, older

Lesson 6

Page 38
Entries in Venn diagrams will vary.

Page 39
Paragraphs will vary.

Lesson 7

Page 40
Entries in Venn diagrams will vary.

Page 41
Comparisons will vary.

Lesson 8

Page 42
Topic ideas will vary.
Entries in idea webs will vary.

Page 43
Methods of organization and paragraphs
   will vary.

Page 44
Revisions will vary.

Page 45
Published descriptive paragraphs will vary.

Answer Key

Chapter 4

Lesson 1

Page 48

Main character: Morgan

Possible details: He is not on Earth. He is on the way to Monroe Flats. He is the Environment Manager for a colony. He likes to walk. He uses a Telewave to communicate.

Other character: the Chairman

Possible details: He speaks in "smooth tones." He has Morgan's respect.

Setting: on a planet other than Earth

Possible setting details: quiet, empty, craters, hard ground, gray dusty sand

Problem: The main character sees tracks and cannot identify their source.

Main character's action: He follows the tracks to investigate.

Dialogue (possible answers):

Main character: He speaks respectfully to the Chairman.

Other character: The Chairman does not chit-chat; he is business-like.

Sensory details: quietness, "walking on hard ground," "churning and making noise," empty, "gray, dusty sand," "like a person who shies away from a snake," "swishy trail," "smooth tones," buzzing

Page 49

Titles and settings will vary.

Lesson 2

Page 50

Information from passage: The main character has been in this place for 472 days. It's a very quiet place. It is not Earth. The ground is hard, and the character is walking. A colony, which has a generator, is in the distance.

Mood or feeling (possible responses):

serious, a "quiet" feeling, thoughtful

Words that convey mood: *quietness, empty*

Responses will vary.

Page 51

Paragraphs will vary.

Lesson 3

Page 52

Characters listed will vary.

"The Colony" character details (possible answers):

The setting is not on Earth—narrator reveals information.

The character's job is to run tests on soil and atmosphere—narrator reveals information.

The main character's name is Morgan—other character's words reveal information

Morgan respects the Chairman—character's words reveal information

Morgan is not timid—character's actions reveal information

Page 53

Responses and paragraphs will vary.

Lesson 4

Page 54

Chairman: He is either excited or angry about Morgan being out alone.

Kip: He respects the Chairman.

Page 55

"I wonder why the Chairman is so upset," said Kip.

The Chairman yelled, "Morgan should never have gone that far out!"

"Is the transport module ready yet?" he asked.

Dialogue will vary.

Answer Key

Chapter 3 continued

Lesson 5

Page 57
Responses will vary.

Chapter 4

Lesson 6

Page 58
Responses will vary.
Realistic story ideas will vary.

Page 59
Responses will vary.
Science fiction story ideas will vary.

Lesson 7

Page 60
Character details in idea webs will vary.

Page 61
Story maps will vary.

Page 62
Drafts will vary.

Page 64
Revisions will vary.

Chapter 5

Lesson 1

Page 66
Persuasive examples will vary.

Page 67
Persuasive articles will vary.

Lesson 2

Page 68
Explanation of persuasive examples will vary.

Page 69
Circled opinion signal words (in text on page 68): *never, like, believe, think, hope*
Possible facts from Mariah's article:
Some classes will never again be offered at OMS.; Students will take consumer science.; Former home ec rooms now house computer labs and a video lab.; Proposed class offerings involve multimedia presentations, digital images, online research.; Parents work full-time and have less time to teach cooking skills.
Possible opinions from Mariah's article:
Changes to the home ec department are "drastic."; Cooking is old-fashioned.; It wasn't a good idea to do away with cooking classes.; Cooking is important.
Fact from Tisha's article:
New classes involve creating and using digital images.
Circled opinion signal words: think, always, believe
Possible opinions from Tisha's article:
Students may cite any sentence except the one about the content of the new classes.
Students' personal opinions will vary.

Answer Key

Chapter 5 continued

Lesson 3

Page 70
Issues will vary.

Page 71
The emotional appeal in Mr. Scariffe's letter is aimed at strong positive feelings that people have about education and hard work. It also gets at strong feelings people have about people who drop out of school or seem to be "wasting" their education.
Letters to the editor will vary.

Lesson 4

Page 72
Comfortable is how the printing company wants you to feel about using their services.
Just because "other people" are drinking Kool Water, you should, too.
Audience for car seat ad: parents
I would need to appeal to their strong feelings about safety and comfort for their children.

Page 73
Slogans and advertisements will vary.

Lesson 5

Page 74
Reasons why there should be a Spanish class:
1) It would be a valuable addition to course offerings.
2) The need to speak and understand Spanish increases as the Hispanic population in the United States increases.
3) Improved communication will help English-speaking and Spanish-speaking communities get along.
4) Many jobs and opportunities are available for people who speak both English and Spanish.
5) And, educators agree that the best time to learn a language is when you are young.
6) Statistics also indicate that learning a language can teach skills that transfer to other classes, resulting in better grades and test scores.

Page 75
Prewriting notes and letters will vary.

Lesson 6

Page 77
Letters of complaint will vary.

Lesson 7

Page 78
Students' complaints will vary.
Entries in idea webs will vary.

Page 79
Students' organizational notes will vary.

Page 80
Drafts will vary.

Page 82
Revisions will vary.

Answer Key

Chapter 6

Lesson 1

Page 84
Responses will vary.

Page 85
Order words underlined in paragraph:
First, as soon as, Then
Responses will vary.

Lesson 2

Page 86
Circled cause-and-effect words: *so, as a result*
Possible causes and effects:
Cause: Plates rub against each other. Effect: Plates buckle or overlap.
Cause: Plates buckle or overlap. Effect: Surface of Earth shakes or heaves.

Page 87
Possible causes and effects:
Cause: Brian does an emergency landing. Effect: He is hurt and alone.
Cause: Brian builds shelter and makes spears. Effect: He is protected.
Cause: Brian makes spears. Effect: He is able to obtain fish for food.
Cause: Brian uses his wits. Effect: He survives.
Responses will vary.

Lesson 3

Page 88
Circled words in paragraph: *because, As a result, Because*
Possible causes and effects:
Cause: There was an oil slick. Effect: Marsh's car went out of control.
Cause: Marsh went out of control. Effect: His vehicle left the roadway.

Cause: The guardrail is being replaced. Effect: A temporary guardrail was in place.
Cause: The temporary guardrail did not stop the vehicle. Effect: The vehicle went down an embankment and lodged in a tree.
Cause: The temporary railing did not work. Effect: An investigation will be performed.

Page 89
Responses will vary.
Paragraphs will vary.

Lesson 4

Page 90
Bar graphs will vary.

Page 91
Visual aids will vary.

Lesson 5

Page 92
Underlined words in paragraph: *First, down, end, bottom, straight, past, Then, turn right, down, end, left, beyond*

Page 93
Directions will vary.

Lesson 6

Page 94
Responses and entries in idea webs will vary.

Page 95
Entries in organizational chart will vary.

Page 96
Instructions will vary.

Page 98
Revisions will vary.

Answer Key

Chapter 7

Lesson 1

Page 101
Circled transition words (in text on page 100): *but, because, so, then, Then, and, Next, Finally,*
Topic explorations will vary.

Lesson 2

Page 102
Replacement words or phrases will vary.

Page 103
Product reviews will vary.

Lesson 3

Page 104
almanac
web site; online encyclopedia
print encyclopedia
atlas
newspaper
dictionary
online encyclopedia; web site

Page 105
yes
no
yes
no

Lesson 4

Page 107
Entries on note cards will vary.

Lesson 5

Page 109
Outlines will vary.

Lesson 6

Page 111
Bibliographic entries will vary, but must follow the formats given.

Lesson 7

Page 113
Entries in chart will vary.

Lesson 8

Page 114
Entries in chart will vary.

Page 115
Entries in chart will vary.

Page 116
Drafts will vary.

Page 118
Revisions will vary.